HIKE
THE EAST BAY

Hike. Contemplate what makes you happy and what makes you happier still. Follow a trail or blaze a new one. **Hike.** Think about what you can do to expand your life and someone else's. **Hike.** Slow down. Gear up. **Hike.** Connect with friends. Re-connect with nature.

Hike. Shed stress. Feel blessed. **Hike** to remember. **Hike** to forget. **Hike** for recovery. **Hike** for discovery. **Hike.** Enjoy the beauty of providence. **Hike.** Share the way, The Hiker's Way, on the long and winding trail we call life.

HIKE
THE EAST BAY

BY
JOHN MCKINNEY

TheTrailmaster.com

HIKE the East Bay by John McKinney
HIKE the East Bay ©2019 The Trailmaster, Inc. All rights reserved. Manufactured in the United States of America. No part of this book may be used or reproduced in any manner whatsoever without written permission except in the case of brief quotations embodied in articles and reviews.

ISBN-13: 978-0-934161-84-8

Book Design by Lisa DeSpain
Cartography by Brandi Webber
Hike Series Editor: Cheri Rae

Photo Credits: California State Parks, p. 91; Jenn Clarke, p. 33; East Bay Regional Park District, p. 15; National Park Service, pp. 67, 75, 106; Miguel Veira, p. 22

Published by Olympus Press and The Trailmaster, Inc. TheTrailmaster.com (Visit our site for a complete listing of all Trailmaster publications, products, and services.)

Although The Trailmaster, Inc. and the author have made every attempt to ensure that information in this book is accurate, they are not responsible for any loss, damage, injury, or inconvenience that may occur to you while using this information. You are responsible for your own safety; the fact that an activity or trail is described in this book does not mean it will be safe for you. Trail conditions can change from day to day; always check local conditions and know your limitations.

Contents

Introduction 9
The East Bay 17

I Berkeley and Oakland Hills

Tilden Regional Park 25
   De Anza Lake, Botanic Garden, and other pleasures of the East Bay's favorite recreation area.

Tilden Botanic Garden 28
   A splendid walk and opportunity to explore native plants from all over California.

Wildcat Canyon Regional Park 31
   Jewel Lake, Wildcat Peak, and the Bay Area at your feet.

Huckleberry Botanic Preserve 35
   A walk on the wild side of the Berkeley Hills on Huckleberry Nature Path.

Sibley Volcanic Preserve 39
   Ramble Round Top and experience a "Volcano by the Bay."

Redwood Regional Park 43
   Oakland wasn't named for its redwoods; this park is—for good reason.

Joaquin Miller Park 47
   Remembering "the Poet of the Sierras" in a preserve filled with redwoods and other trees.

LEONA CANYON ... 51
    Paws to consider. Hikers and dogs love this gentle wooded canyon.

ANTHONY CHABOT REGIONAL PARK ... 55
    Chabot: rhymes with meadow. Take a hike through Grass Valley.

II Parks East and South

BLACK DIAMOND MINES ... 61
    West Virginia in the East Bay? Explore rugged hills and a time when coal was king.

JOHN MUIR NATIONAL HISTORIC SITE ... 65
    Tour the famed naturalist's home; hike Mt. Wanda, named for his daughter.

BRIONES REGIONAL PARK ... 69
    Panoramas from Mott Peak, room to roam for cows and hikers.

LAS TRAMPAS REGIONAL WILDERNESS ... 73
    Hike up Rocky Ridge and around a challenging "hiker's park."

EUGENE O'NEILL NATIONAL HISTORIC SITE ... 77
    Take a trail to, and tour of, Tao House, home to America's most distinguished playwright of the 20th century.

MISSION PEAK ... 81
    Get a unique perspective on Silicon Valley from popular pathway and peak.

SUNOL WILDERNESS REGIONAL PARK ... 85
    Little Yosemite, Indian Joe Nature Trail, and a wilderness retreat.

Mt. Diablo

MOUNT DIABLO SUMMIT ... 89
    Classic "Grand Loop" offers grand views of—and from—mighty mountain.

MOUNT DIABLO SLOPES ... 93
    Mitchell Canyon, Eagle Peak, and Diablo's diverse ecology.

III By the Bay

POINT PINOLE 99
  Hike to a pier, bird-watching spots, and vista points on Bay View Trail.

MILLER-KNOX REGIONAL SHORELINE 103
  Hike Ferry Point Loop Trail, one of the most scenic and historic stretches of the Bay Trail.

ROSIE THE RIVETER WWII NATIONAL HISTORICAL PARK 107
  Walk Kaiser Shipyard 3 Trail and learn about the women and men who worked on the home front to make Victory ships—and victory—possible.

BROOKS ISLAND 111
  An island adventure! Sign up for a kayak/hiking tour of this natural treasure.

MCGLAUGHLIN EASTSHORE STATE PARK 115
  Highly urbanized this coast is, and highly popular, too—particularly around Point Isabel, a de facto dog park.

CROWN BEACH 119
  Swimmers appreciate the (relatively) warm water, hikers appreciate the sand dunes, bird sanctuary and beach.

MARTIN LUTHER KING JR. REGIONAL SHORELINE 123
  Bayside trails offer close-up views of birds, birds, and more birds.

HAYWARD REGIONAL SHORELINE 127
  Hike along narrow levees and across footbridges as you explore this park, one of the best spots in the East Bay to view shorebirds.

COYOTE HILLS REGIONAL PARK 131
  Hike small hills (with big views) and scenic shores of sprawling marshland.

SAN FRANCISCO BAY NATIONAL WILDLIFE REFUGE 135
  Tidelands Trail tours nation's largest wildlife refuge.

ABOUT THE AUTHOR 142

The East Bay beckons hikers with one of the best regional park trail networks in the nation.

EVERY TRAIL TELLS A STORY.

Introduction

The East Bay leads the way. With its park system. With its trail system. And with its exemplary leadership and citizen action over many decades that has created a collection of parklands and trails admired nationwide.

The East Bay is a great place to take a hike. For good reason. For *many* good reasons. Begin with a great variety of greenery and scenery. Add a world-class park system, fine trails, and four-season hiking.

And add a rich diversity of fellow hikers of all ages, shapes and sizes. The East Bay is one of the most ethnically and culturally diverse regions in the country and the hiking experience is much enriched by sharing the trail with hikers from literally all walks of life.

The Trailmaster has attended his share of park symposiums and trail conferences and witnessed the high regard land managers and trail enthusiasts have for East Bay parks and trails—and the people behind them. On a more personal note, I have listened to the sad stories of friends, longtime residents, who took jobs in other parts of California and in other states, and who were dismayed to find the quality and quantity of hiking trails near their new homes was far inferior to those they had enjoyed in the East Bay. Sigh.

You mean other parts of the country don't have parks and trails like those in the East Bay?

Indeed not.

More formally known as the eastern region of the San Francisco Bay Area, the East Bay is usually defined as the two counties of Alameda and Contra Costa. *HIKE the East Bay* shares a sampling of the best day hikes in the two counties. Given the large number of parks and stellar hikes in the East Bay, it was challenging to say the least to select the "best" hikes.

The hikes described in this pocket guide are surely enjoyable, even memorable. When I think of my own hikes in the East Bay, I'm filled with happy memories. Here's one from a hike in the Berkeley Hills:

I heard the sweet singing before I saw the singers.

"Valerieeeee, valerahhhhh…"

Through mist-enshrouded Wildcat Canyon trooped a platoon of kindergartners, splashing in the puddles and singing in the rain: "Valerieeee, valerah-ha-ha-ha-ha-ha…"

Rain on their parade served only to increase the pleasure of the dozen little hikers and their obviously

Introduction

fun-loving teacher from a nearby elementary school. Storm clouds had sealed off the park from all sight and sounds of civilization; the five-year olds may well have imagined they were trekking in a remote wilderness rather than a canyon located less than a mile as the red-tailed hawk flies from Interstate 80.

It's not grand panoramas, but little trailside sights that impress children and, in Wildcat Canyon Regional Park, there is much to capture a child's imagination: a banana slug crawling over a mossy log, a newt slithering across the trail, frogs croaking, and a variety of songbirds maintaining a subdued, but steady calling from their perches in the trees.

Not long after encountering the little hikers in their brightly-colored raincoats, the rain stopped and, from a perch atop San Pablo Ridge, I watched the cloudy curtain part and reveal much of the Bay Area at my feet: Mt. Tamalpais, the Marin Headlands, the San Francisco skyline, the Golden Gate Bridge, lots of San Francisco Bay, Mt. Diablo.

Another great day hiking the East Bay! You're sure to have lots of them yourself when you hit the trail here.

East Bay Regional Park District administers a system of regional parks that comprise the largest urban regional park system in the U.S. EBRPD beckons the hiker with 65 parks, 120 thousand acres of parkland, and more than 1,250(!) miles of trail.

By design, the district's network of parks and trails is intended to put parkland within reach (15 to 30 minutes max by car or public transit) of each and every resident of Alameda and Contra Costa counties.

Parks vary greatly in size, scenery and recreational opportunities. The park system includes a former coal mine, dynamite-making factory, Nike missile sites, farms, ranches, quarries, cut-over timberland, and wild land never developed because it proved too steep or inaccessible.

Some parks have lots of facilities (collectively East Bay parks boast 3,806 picnic tables!) while others are "hiker parks" with few or no amenities. Take a walk on the wild side at parks with wilderness in their names: Las Trampas Wilderness Park and Sunol Regional Wilderness Park. Or take your dog on a hike: EBRPD is one of the few park systems in the country that permit dogs off-leash on hundreds of miles of trail.

Hikers love the classic parks in the Berkeley-Oakland Hills: Tilden Regional Park, Wildcat Canyon Regional Park, Huckleberry Botanic Regional Preserve, Sibley Volcanic Regional Preserve, Redwood Regional Park. Those hikers who enjoy coastal trails can choose from a collection of parks along the bay from Coyote Hills Regional Park near Fremont to Point Pinole Regional Shoreline near Richmond.

Introduction

Mount Diablo, a landmark for the East Bay and well beyond, is regarded as one of the gems of the California State Parks system. Mount Diablo State Park is awesomely hiker-friendly—surprising perhaps, considering one can drive to the top of Mt. Diablo and the most obvious foot-powered park users on weekend mornings are colorfully clad cyclists pedaling up and zooming down the mountain.

The National Park Service has a presence in the East Bay, too. At John Muir National Historic Site, tour the great naturalist's home and hike around his former ranch. Marvel at the abundant birdlife as you hike around San Francisco Bay National Wildlife Refuge, under the stewardship of the U.S. Fish and Wildlife Service.

East Bay landmark Mission Peak is visible from many points in Silicon Valley.

The region's long-distance trails are an added attraction for the hiker. EBRPD maintains numerous trails that link one park to another, like Briones to Las Trampas Trail and Black Diamond to Mt. Diablo Trail.

East Bay Skyline National Trail extends across the hills of the East Bay, connecting regional parks and serving up fabulous views of San Francisco Bay. The 31-mile long trail begins at Wildcat Canyon Regional Park in Richmond and extends through Tilden Regional Park, Sibley Volcanic Regional Preserve, Huckleberry Botanic Regional Preserve, Redwood Regional Park and Anthony Chabot Regional Park.

A portion of San Francisco Bay Trail, a planned (and 75 percent completed) 500-mile walking and cycling path around the entire San Francisco Bay, traverses numerous East Bay shoreline parks. Bay Area Ridge Trail is a planned (and about two-thirds completed) 550-mile multi-use trail along the hills and ridgelines ringing the San Francisco Bay Area. Large segments of the trail in Alameda and Contra Costa counties have been completed.

The East Bay boasts one of the best climates in the U.S. for year-around hiking. The rainy season extends from November through April, and rainy days can cancel your hiking plans. (Also rain-soaked trails, especially steep ones, can become difficult, even impassable, and can force a change in plans.) Hot summer days (particularly in the inland parks) are about the only other weather restrictions on taking a hike.

Oakland's nickname "bright side of the Bay" is not just hype; indeed it does have a lot of days with sunny skies—particularly in comparison to its famously foggy neighbor across the bay—and its temperature usually reads at least five degrees warmer than San Francisco. East Bay cities and parklands located further inland have even warmer temperatures.

More so than in other communities, East Bay residents seem to know that hiking is good—and good for you, and have been pioneers in the promotion of hiking for improved health and fitness. EBRPD has long sponsored an annual "Trails Challenge," designed to get people to take a series of hikes and enjoy the mental physical and spiritual well-being that comes from time on the trail. Healthcare provider

Take the Trails Challenge, an annual program sponsored by the East Bay Regional Park District.

Kaiser Permanente sponsors the Trails Challenge and other hiking for health programs in the East Bay.

Hiking for health and fitness: yet another example of how the East Bay leads the way.

Hike smart, reconnect with nature, and have a great time on the trail.

Hike On.

John McKinney

The East Bay

Geography

In 1851, Mt. Diablo's summit, long a landmark for California explorers, was established as the official base point for California land surveys. Even today, Mt. Diablo's baseline and meridian lines are used in legal descriptions of much California real estate. Geographers claim we can see more of the earth's surface from the top of Mt. Diablo than from any other peak in the world with only one exception: Africa's 19,340-foot Mt. Kilimanjaro.

With a population of more than 2.5 million, the East Bay is the most populous region in the San Francisco Bay area. Oakland is the largest city of the East Bay, which includes cities all along the eastern shores of San Francisco Bay and San Pablo Bay. The East Bay has half a dozen cities with populations of more than 100 thousand: Berkeley, Richmond, Hayward, Fremont, Antioch and Concord.

The park system and trails network has similarly expanded eastward.

While heavily urbanized and suburbanized, the East Bay is comparatively park rich compared to most other population centers.

Conservation History

The East Bay Regional Parks District was founded in 1934. Two of its visionary founders were hiking enthusiast Robert Sibley and Charles Lee Tilden, both of whom had parks named after them. Forward-thinking leaders included William Penn Mott, who served as general manager of the EBRPD from 1962 to 1967. During his tenure, park acreage doubled and the number of parks in the system tripled. He later went on to become California State Parks director

Mt. Diablo State Park opened in 1931; over the years conservationists have successfully quadrupled the amount of preserved land around the mighty mountain.

and National Park Service Director. Hulet Hornbeck served with distinction as Chief of Land Acquisition for the EBRPD from 1965 through 1985, and was well-known locally, statewide, and nationwide for his many years of volunteer efforts on behalf of trails.

The East Bay citizenry has steadfastly supported the park system from the district's creation during the depths of the Great Depression to today. Community support has been unwavering over the years—voting for bond measures, and contributing countless volunteer hours. Thanks to top leadership and an engaged public, the EBRPD is the largest, and most innovative, regional park system in the U.S.

In 1931, the upper slopes of Mt. Diablo were preserved in a (rather small) state park. In later years, the mountain's lower slopes were added to the park, thanks in large measure to efforts made by Save Mt. Diablo, a local conservation organization. Today Mt. Diablo State Park consists of some 20,000 acres of oak woodland, grassland and chaparral. Now circling Diablo are more than three dozen parks and preserves, totaling some 90,000 acres.

Natural History

The East Bay's many habitats—including bay shoreline, salt marsh, chaparral, grassland, riparian and redwood forest—support more than 350 species of birds.

Prevailing winds blow from west to east and influence what grows where. Moist Pacific air first reaches the Oakland-Berkeley Hills; other hills in Alameda and Contra Costa counties diminish the winds so that the region's valleys get progressively hotter to the east. Flora and fauna vary from one microclimate to another.

Oaks are everywhere—from Oak-land to all across Alameda and Contra Costa counties. The oak is the iconic tree of the East Bay and fitting symbol of the East Bay Regional Park District. The hiker might identify half a dozen varieties along the trails: three deciduous species (valley, blue, black) and three evergreen (coast live, canyon live and interior live).

The East Bay's remaining redwoods are a reminder of a time when great groves of the giants grew in the region. All first-growth redwoods were logged by the end of the 19th century, but impressive stands of second-growth redwoods now thrive in Redwood Regional Park and Joaquin Miller Park.

From Rocky Ridge in Las Trampas Wilderness Park to Grass Valley in Anthony Chabot Regional Park to parklands all across the East Bay, wildflower displays are often awesome. Check the EBRPD site for more information.

Administration

East Bay Regional Park District, located at 2950 Peralta Oaks Court in Oakland, administers 65 parks. Call 1-888-EBPARKS or 1-888-327-2757 EBRPD's excellent web site (ebparks.org) has all the latest information on the parks, downloadable maps, wildflower lists and photos and much more. The Regional Parks Foundation assists the EBRPD in its mission to provide recreation for all. Learn more about its programs at regionalparksfoundation.org.

Joaquin Miller Park is owned by the city of Oakland. More info: 510-615-5566

Don Edwards San Francisco National Wildlife Refuge call 510-792-0222 or visit fws.gov/refuge/don_edwards_san_francisco_bay/.

For info about Mount Diablo State Park, call 925-837-2525 or visit parks.ca.gov and the Mount Diablo Interpretive Association mdia.org

To learn more about visiting John Muir National Historic Site, call 925-228-8860 or visit nps.gov/jomu.

Transit and Trails

Many parks and trails are accessible by public transit. Visit the EBRPD site (ebparks.org) or Transit and Trails (transitandtrails.org).

Trails lead through oaks in the Oakland-Berkeley hills—and redwoods, too!

EVERY TRAIL TELLS A STORY.

I
BERKELEY AND OAKLAND HILLS

HIKE ON.

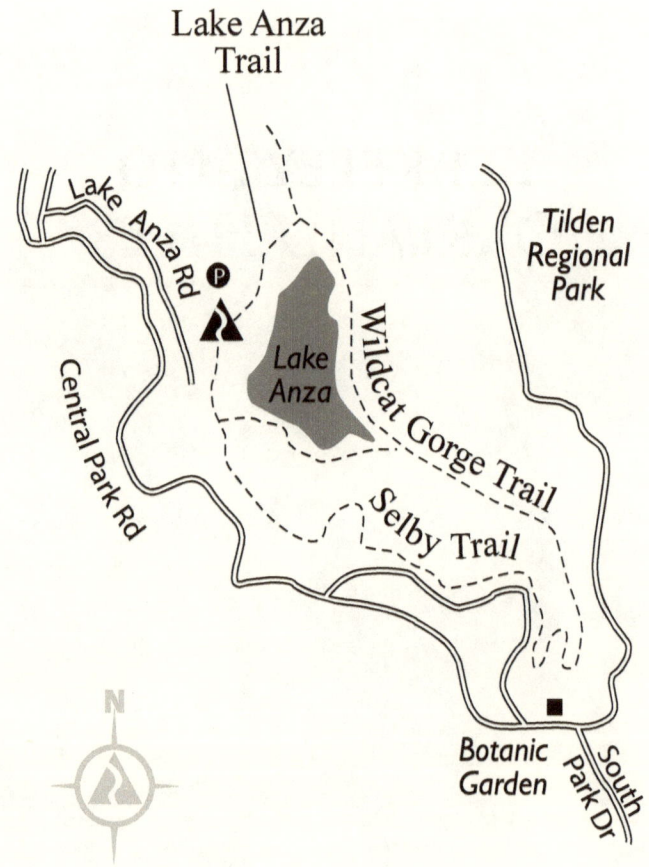

Tilden Regional Park
Wildcat Gorge, Selby Trails

1.5-mile loop

Mention "Tilden Park" to an East Bay resident, past or present, and it invariably brings forth a pleasant memory: the antique merry-go-round, the botanic garden, the golf course, Lake Anza with its popular beach.

Hikers have a good time in Tilden, too. This jaunt on Wildcat Gorge and Selby Trails offers a tour of two Tilden attractions—Lake Anza and the botanic garden. High on the northwest slope are the headwaters of Wildcat Creek, which flows through the Regional Park Botanic Garden into Lake Anza—eventually emptying into San Pablo Bay a bit north of the Richmond-San Rafael Bridge.

Don't miss the botanic garden, which features the native plants of California from the mountains to the deserts to the sea. Add a mile—and a couple hours—to this hike with a garden walk. As a garden publication puts it: "Imagine 160,000 square miles of California set in a garden that can be walked in a day."

The park is full of contrasts: wild, brushy slopes and irrigated lawns, seasonal creeks and artificial lakes. Tilden is no wilderness, but does promote ecological values and learning with classes and exhibits at the Environmental Education Center.

Tilden is tucked in a valley, bounded by San Pablo Ridge to the east and Berkeley Hills to the west. Shading trails and picnic areas are native forests of oak and bay, as well as planted stands of eucalyptus and Monterey pine.

Park namesake Charles Lee Tilden was a driving force behind East Bay parks for the 1930s. It was during this Depression-decade that the Civilian Conservation Corps constructed Tilden Park's trail system; it includes something for everyone from a mile-long, self-guided nature trail around Jewel Lake to a segment of Skyline National Trail, that 31-mile long East Bay gem.

DIRECTIONS: From Highway 24, just east of Caldecott Tunnel, exit on Fish Ranch Road and head west 0.8 mile to Grizzly Peak Boulevard. Make a right and go 1.3 miles to South Park Drive, go right again to intersect Central Park Road opposite the Botanic Garden. Head left and in 0.3 mile take the turnoff to the right to Lake Anza and parking lots.

THE HIKE: Head east on the paved path and descend toward Lake Anza, joining Lake Anza Trail. Cross a bridge over Wildcat Creek then walk a dirt path across the top of the dam, turning right to stay with the lakeshore path. Meet Wildcat Gorge Trail and follow the narrow and rocky path along the creek amidst ferns and dogwood, eucalyptus and redwood. Cross a bridge over the creek and hike west past the botanic garden.

Wildcat Gorge Trail dead-ends about a mile from the trailhead at a junction with Selby Trail. Continue onto Selby Trail and descend toward the Lake Anza's beach area. Merge onto Lake Anza Trail, travel past a grove of redwoods to the bathhouse and walk the paved path back to the parking lot.

The loop around Lake Anza is a great introduction to Tilden Park.

Tilden Regional Park Botanic Garden

This little garden is big on California.

Other states may have deserts, mountains, valleys, islands or long coastlines, but only California has all of these environments. And all these environments are represented—10 geographically based sections in 10 acres—in Tilden Regional Park Botanic Garden.

While considerably smaller than better-known botanic gardens at UC Berkeley and in San Francisco's Golden Gate Park, Tilden Garden has much to offer, particularly when it comes to its displays of native California flora. Tree-lovers will be delighted by a walk through the redwoods and by the garden's comprehensive collections of oaks and conifers.

Other extensive collections include native California grasses, manzanita, and aquatic plants. The garden is also a safe haven for some 300 plants on the California Native Plant Society's "Rare and Endangered" list.

Begin your exploration of California at the garden visitor center, pick up a brochure/map and head for the Sierra, Channel Islands, or Pacific rain forest.

Meander the walkways and across footbridges over Wildcat Creek to reach exceptionally well re-created Golden State landscapes named Santa Lucia, Valley-Foothill, and Shasta-Klamath.

"Imagine 160,000 square miles of California set in a garden that can be walked in a day," garden boosters suggest. Indeed!

Something is blooming every month at the garden, which is open every day from 8 a.m. to 5 p.m. The garden is lightly visited, even on busy weekends in the park. And admission is free.

DIRECTIONS: The main garden entrance is at the junction of Wildcat Canyon Road and South Park Drive. Look for a side entrance off Anza View Road. Park in the free parking lot across Wildcat Road, and be very careful crossing the road (blind turn, fast traffic) to the garden.

Trails lead through California's diverse environments in the botanical garden.

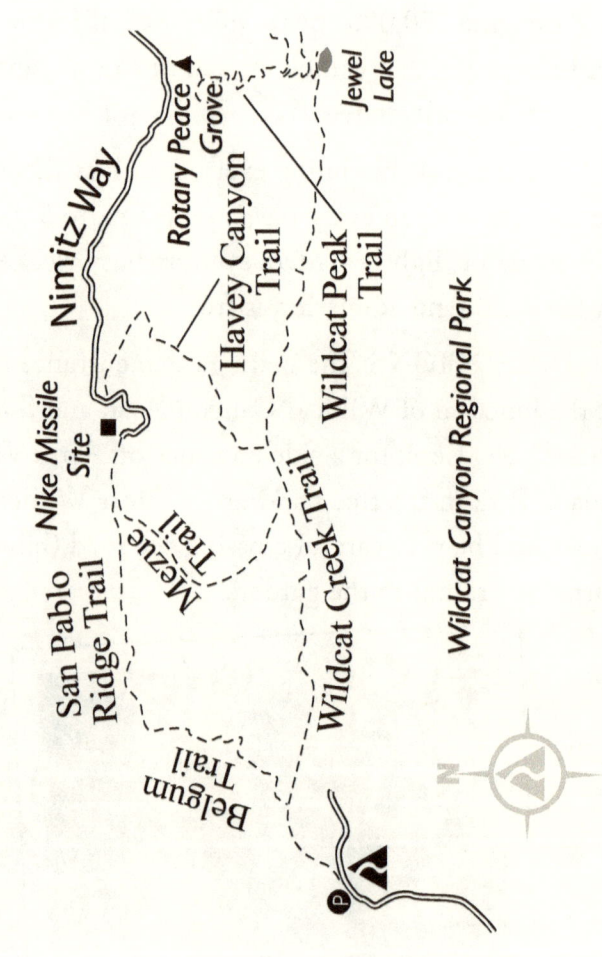

WILDCAT CANYON

WILDCAT CREEK, WILDCAT PEAK, NIMITZ WAY, SAN PABLO RIDGE, BELGUM TRAILS

From Alvarado Park to Jewel Lake is 8 miles round trip; to Wildcat Peak is 11 miles round trip with 900-foot elevation gain.

Wildcat is the flip side of adjacent Tilden Park; it's far less developed, far less visited. Trails offer the only access to its wide meadows, remote canyons, tall ridges.

A climb to park high points—Wildcat Peak (1,211 feet), an old Nike missile site, and San Pablo Ridge—puts much of the Bay Area at your feet: Mt. Tamalpais, Marin Headlands, San Francisco skyline, Golden Gate Bridge, lots of San Francisco Bay, Mt. Diablo.

DIRECTIONS: From westbound I-80 exit on McBryde and from eastbound I-80 in Richmond, take the Solano Avenue exit and head east on Amador Street. At the second stop sign, turn right on McBryde, continuing to a stop sign and the entrance to Alvarado Park. Continue straight onto Park Avenue and travel 0.25 mile to the long parking lot for Wildcat Canyon Regional Park.

THE HIKE: Begin hiking along Wildcat Creek Trail (a wide paved road early on) lined with oak, eucalyptus and toyon. After a short jaunt, intersect Belgum Trail. (If you only want a short hike, hoof it 0.7 mile up Belgum Trail to a vista point for a grand San Francisco Bay panorama.)

Continue along a handsome section of Wildcat Creek Trail. Under one of the frequent blankets of fog that seals off the park from all sight and sound of civilization, hikers may imagine they are trekking in a remote wilderness rather than in a canyon located less than a mile from Interstate 80 and the city of Richmond.

At the two-mile mark, pass a junction with Mezue Trail, a path that climbs from the canyon to San Pablo Ridge. After another 0.3 mile, the trail crosses a bridge over Wildcat Creek and soon climbs very briefly to pass junctions with Havey Canyon Trail and Conlon Trail.

Stick with Wildcat Creek Trail and hike another 2 miles to Jewel Lake, a lovely little reservoir along the creek. Turn left on single-track Jewel Lake Trail and in a few hundred feet veer left onto Sylvan Path. Ascend a short 0.5 mile to meet and join Wildcat Peak Trail.

Ascend amidst eucalyptus groves and brush on the switchbacking trail. (Please don't cut switchbacks). Reach the handsome stone lookout and Rotary Club Peace Grove, sequoias dedicated to the world's peacemakers.

After enjoying the summit views, rejoin Wildcat Peak Trail for a final 0.3 mile to meet Nimitz Way. Turn left on the paved road. At the 6.2-mile mark, pass a junction with Conlon Trail and the meadow that once hosted a Nike missile site. At 8 miles out, hike by the associated Nike radar site (as evidenced by stone foundations atop a hill).

Happily the pavement ends here and you continue on dirt San Pablo Ridge Trail for another 1.5 miles to meet Belgum Trail, which descends 1.1 miles to the paved part of Wildcat Creek Trail. Retrace your steps a last 0.4 mile to the trailhead.

Wildcat Regional Park: A breath of fresh air, wide-open spaces and big sky.

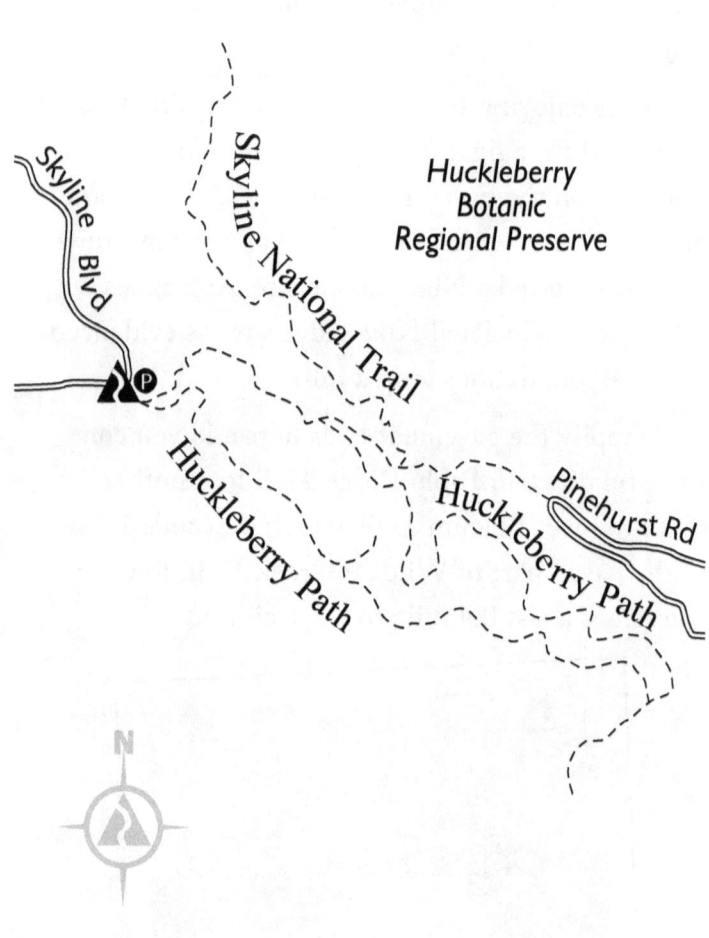

HUCKLEBERRY BOTANIC REGIONAL PRESERVE

HUCKLEBERRY PATH

1.7 miles loop through preserve

Enjoy a self-guided nature trail amidst the many flowering (and fruiting) plants at Huckleberry Botanic Regional Preserve. Look for thimbleberries early in the summer, and the pink-flowered currant in late winter/early spring.

The preserve's namesake huckleberries bear fruit in late summer and early fall. During the summer when other parks in the hills are hot and brown, the preserve is a shady and green retreat.

The preserve's rare plant communities, which evolved in isolation during a time when the climate was wetter, have been likened to those on the Channel Islands located off the coast of Santa Barbara. Its cool microclimate is a result of its northern exposure on the backside of the Berkeley Hills and its location—directly across from the Golden Gate—and that means lots of summer fog.

Without being overly academic or making you feel like you're listening to a high school botany class lecture, the 17-stop Huckleberry Path helps you appreciate this island in time. Turns out the huckleberry is one tough plant; it has survived for so long, in part because it overgrows and kills chinquapin and manzanita. Who knew?

About a half-mile or so of Huckleberry Path is part of a trio of famed pathways: Skyline National Trail, Bay Area Ridge Trail and Anza Trail. You can use this thrice-named trail to make a longer loop of the preserve or travel to Robert Sibley Volcanic Preserve and well beyond.

DIRECTIONS: From Highway 24 in Oakland, just east of the Caldecott Tunnel, exit on Fish Ranch Road and drive 0.8 mile to Grizzly Peak Boulevard. Turn left and proceed 2.4 miles to Skyline Boulevard, turn left and drive 0.5 mile to the Huckleberry Botanic Regional Preserve entry on the left (0.25 mile past Robert Sibley Volcanic Preserve).

THE HIKE: Begin on Huckleberry Path, which soon forks at a signed junction. Stay left and descend switchbacks, arriving at Stop #1 and the first flora identified: madrone. About 0.4 mile along, the path junctions Skyline Trail. Stay right, and begin a mellow ascent amidst ferns and flowering plants.

Just short of a mile out, reach a signed junction and turn right. To add another 0.75 mile to your hike, keep left at the junction with Skyline Trail, hike 0.45 mile, and then go right onto Huckleberry Path Trail and continue another 0.3 mile or so to rejoin the classic nature loop.

All three of the East Bay live oaks grow here, including the common coast live oak and interior live oak, and the uncommon canyon live oak. You can identify this oak by the golden fuzz on the undersides of the leaves, and by the fuzzy golden cups that hold the acorns.

Pass a 0.3 mile side trail leading to Stops 8-9-10 and continue on the now narrow path lined with tall huckleberry thickets. In one open area sneak a view of Mt, Diablo. Reach the final identified plant—pink-flowered currant—and return to the trailhead.

Look for huckleberries along the Huckleberry Path

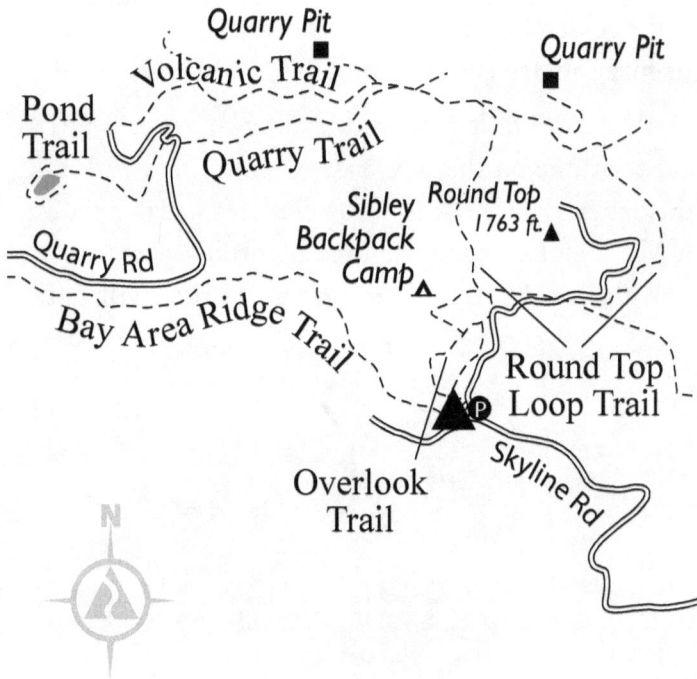

ROBERT SIBLEY VOLCANIC REGIONAL PRESERVE

ROUND TOP LOOP TRAIL

4-mile loop with 400-foot elevation gain.

Great American volcanoes: Lassen Peak, Mt. Shasta, Mt. St. Helens, Mauna Loa and Old Round Top.

Old what? Strange as it seems, the Bay Area had, still has, a volcano. Long extinct Round Top may appear today as little more than a little rounded hill among larger Oakland-Berkeley Hills, but some 10 million years ago it was a mighty volcano that erupted beneath a large lake. The molten lava interior of the mountain then fell into the void left by the explosion.

Robert Sibley Volcanic Regional Preserve displays this odd bit of East Bay geology. Pre-park quarry operations revealed some of the volcano's secrets. A nature trail tells the story of the "Volcano By the Bay" and offers great panoramic views.

A gated road leads to the top of 1,763-foot Round Top, where excellent clear-day vistas unfold of the East Bay and San Francisco Bay. An even better look at the mountain's fiery past, and even better present-day panoramas, can be enjoyed from the Round Top Loop Trail. It's an interpretive path (keyed to a brochure available from the park visitor center) and explains the volcanic outburst and area ecology.

The park boasts more trails. Volcanic Trail offers excellent views and intriguing geological formations. Nearly three miles of East Bay National Skyline Trail crosses the park; you can hike all day north or south to many more East Bay parks.

DIRECTIONS: From Highway 24, northeast of Oakland and just east of the Caldecott Tunnel, exit on Fish Ranch Road. Drive 0.8 mile to Grizzly Peak Boulevard, turn left and proceed 2.5 miles to Skyline Boulevard. Turn left and in one hundred yards turn left into Robert Sibley Volcanic Regional Preserve.

THE HIKE: From the signed trailhead, choose Overlook Trail or Skyline Trail (they meet in 0.25 mile). Follow Skyline Trail 0.2 mile to met the paved road leading to the top of Round Top. If it's a clear day, take the road to the top.

After taking in the views from the summit, descend and turn left on Round Top Loop Trail. The narrow path traverses grasslands, then passes a quarry pit that reveals the interior of the old volcano. A bit past the pit, the loop trail meets Volcanic Trail.

Join Volcanic Trail, which soon offers an impressive view of Mt. Diablo and leads 0.25 mile to a quarry pit that shows lava flows and red cinders—remnants of a volcanic vent.

Two spur trails offer additional perspectives. The leftward path crests a knoll, where the hiker is treated to a fine panorama of the Bay Bridge and San Francisco. Another side path leads to a weird gathering of bay laurel and lava boulders and grants vistas to the north.

Retrace your steps on Volcanic Trail back to Round Top Loop Trail and turn right, closing the loop back to the trailhead.

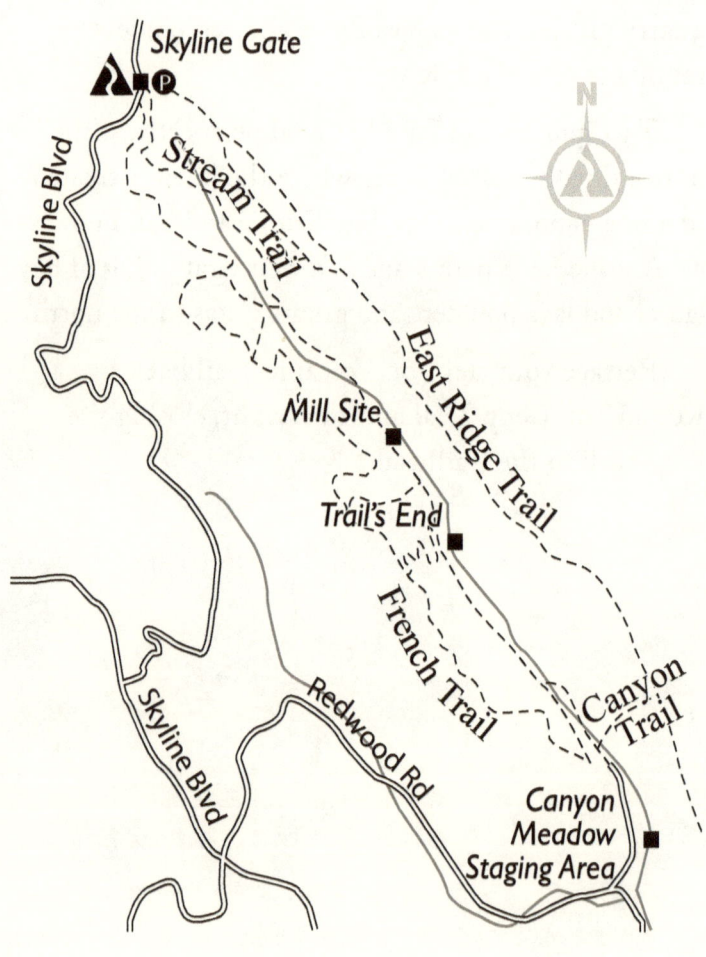

Redwood Regional Park

Stream, Canyon, East Ridge Trails

To Trail's End is 4 miles round trip; loop is 6 miles round trip

Oakland wasn't named for its redwoods, that's for sure. Yet a magnificent redwood forest once thrived at what is now the eastern edge of the metropolis.

During and after the Gold Rush of 1849 most of these Oakland-adjacent redwoods were felled, the logs sawn at nearby mills, and the lumber shipped to build Oakland and San Francisco. How colossal were the coast redwoods that were chopped down? A stump discovered on the slopes of Redwood Peak measured 33 feet in diameter!

Oakland's redwoods are rather removed from other areas of coast redwoods—the Santa Cruz Mountains to the south and the state and national parks on California's north coast—which makes a walk through the towering giants in Redwood Regional Park all the more special.

A second generation of redwoods, now more than 100 years old, tower more than 150 feet tall. Along with the redwoods, the park includes more typical East Bay terrain—grassy meadows as well as an oak and madrone woodland. Nonnative stands of Monterey pine and eucalyptus are also very much a part of the park.

A southeast tour on Stream Trail and a northwest return on East Ridge Trail offers a counter-clockwise tour of the heart of the park and two distinct experiences: the dark redwood forest and the open ridgeline for grand vistas. Stream Trail is closed to bikes from the Skyline trailhead to Trail's End Picnic Area, so for a peaceful jaunt amidst the redwoods, you could make this a 4-mile long out-and-back hike.

DIRECTIONS: From Highway 13 south of Oakland, exit on Joaquin Miller Road and head east to Skyline Boulevard. Turn left and drive north 5 miles to the Skyline Gate Staging Area.

THE HIKE: Join Stream Trail and descend a brushy canyon wall to Redwood Creek. In 0.4 mile, reach Girls Camp, first of many picnic areas en route. Continue the descent to the magnificent redwoods along the deep and shady canyon cut by Redwood Creek. Pass a junction with Tres Sendas (Three Paths) Trail and continue onward through the dark, fern-filled redwood forest. Cross several bridges over Redwood Creek as you wander from bank to bank amidst the tall trees.

Pass more picnic grounds—from Mill Site to Fern Hut to Trail's End. Turn around here or continue on the now-paved Stream Trail past a half-dozen more picnic sites to meet Canyon Trail near Canyon Meadow Staging Area. Join Canyon Trail, a dirt road on the left, and ascend amidst mixed woodland of oak, Monterey pine, bay and scattered redwoods. The trail meets and continues with East Ridge Trail, bending left on the wide dirt road. Enjoy grand vistas as you climb: east to Mt. Diablo and over several surrounding East Bay parklands.

About 5 miles out, pass a junction with Prince Trail. (You could make a brief descent on this path to Stream Trail and retrace your steps to Skyline.) Continue through the pines and eucalyptus woodland back to the trailhead.

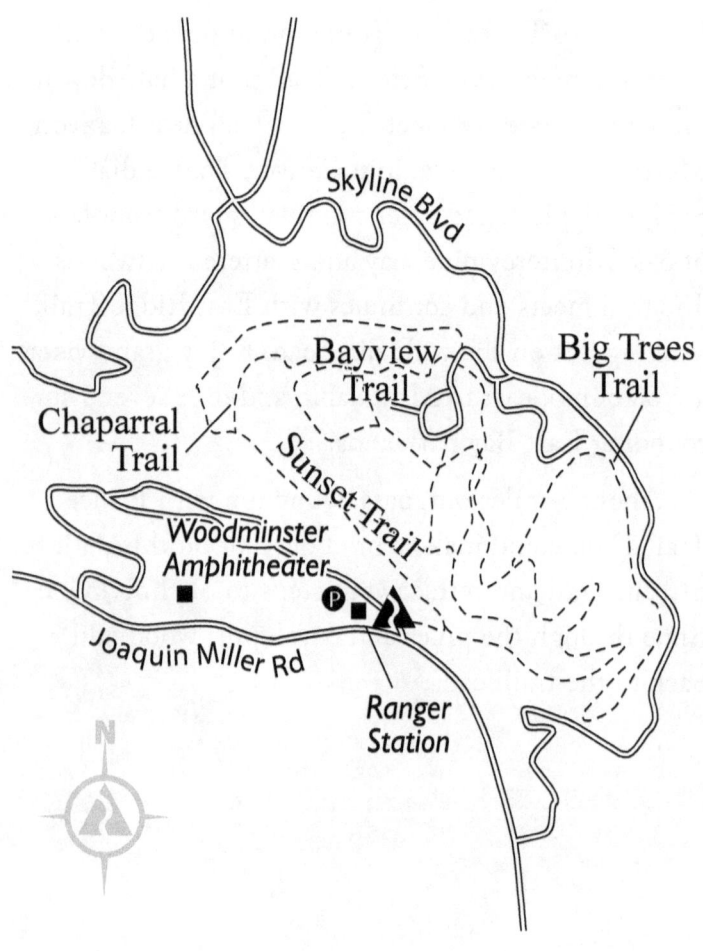

Joaquin Miller Park

Sunset, Sequoia Bay View, Palo Colorado Trails

3.5 mile-loop with 400-foot elevation gain

For the hiker, Joaquin Miller Park, a 500-acre retreat in the Oakland Hills, offers topography and flora similar to nearby, and much better known, Redwood Regional Park. The park is thickly wooded with second-growth redwoods, as well as oaks and Monterey pine.

The park offers picnicking, an off-leash dog area, and a large outdoors amphitheater used to stage plays. Joaquin Miller Ranger Station offers interpretive exhibits that highlight park history and natural features. Woodminster Amphitheater and Cascades (a waterfall feature) were built in 1940 and dedicated to California writers.

During an 1870 visit to the Bay Area, Cincinnatus Hiner had the good fortune to meet California's first poet laureate and Oakland's first librarian, Ina

Coolbrith, who urged him to adopt the pen name Joaquin Miller. The "Poet of the Sierras," as he became known, settled in the Oakland Hills in 1886 and built a home called "The Abbey," now a historic landmark. Joaquin Miller directed the planting of 75,000 trees, many of which still thrive in the park named for this colorful California character.

Sequoia Bay View Trail, popular with local fitness walkers and joggers, is a fairly flat route and the park's main trail. Several short trails branch off of it. This hike visits second-growth redwoods, rare stands that flourish in an urban environment, and offers a pleasant tour of the park.

DIRECTIONS: From its junction with Highway 24, drive south on Highway 13 about 3 miles and exit on Joaquin Miller Road. Turn left, cross back over the highway, and turn right onto Joaquin Miller Road. In 0.8 mile, turn left on Sanborn Drive proceed 0.1 mile. Park along the road near the ranger station or in the lot.

THE HIKE: From the ranger station, walk Sanborn Drive back toward Joaquin Miller Road and look on the left side of the road for the trailhead at a yellow gate. Take (the main) Sunset Trail and stay on it past junctions with other paths and begin a modest ascent of a redwood canyon.

About 0.6 miles out, meet Sequoia Bayview Trail. (Option: A right turn leads to Skyline Boulevard and

Big Trees Trail, which visits the park's largest redwoods and eventually loops back to Sequoia Bay View Trail.) Go left on the wide, flat multi-use trail, meander amidst a mixed woodland of oak, redwood and pine, and contour onto a more open slope with vistas of Oakland and San Francisco. The trail alternates between wooded and open landscapes, passes junctions with Big Trees, Fern Ravine and Wild Rose trails.

At a signed junction at the 2-mile mark, join the first of several trails to make a loop: turn left on Chaparral Trail, descend 0.3 mile and turn left on Sunset Trail, soon meeting Palos Colorado Trail and turning right. Cross a bridge and turn left onto Sinawik Trail, soon meeting Sunset Trail and going right. Walk across a meadow to a gate at Sanborn Drive, turn right, and return to the trailhead.

Poet of the Sierras, Joaquin Miller, remembered in his namesake park.

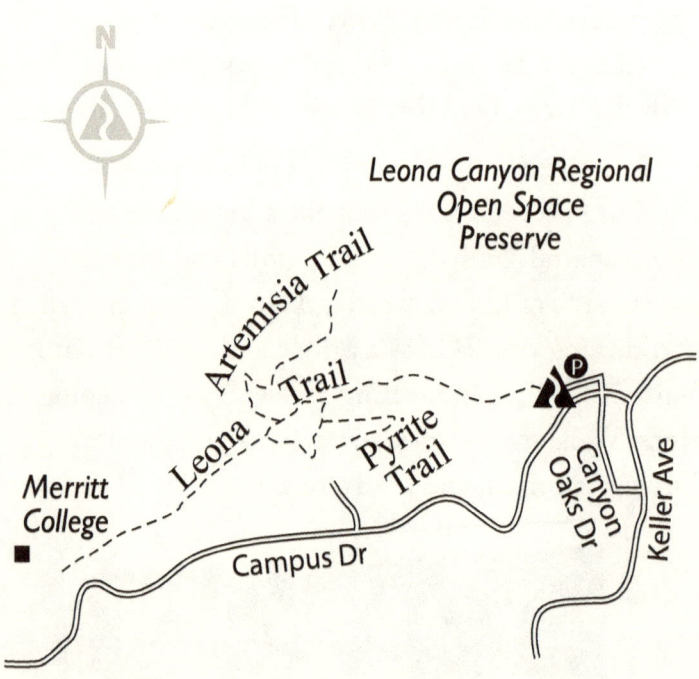

Leona Canyon

Leona Trail

To Merritt College is 2.7 miles with 450-foot elevation gain

Tucked between Merritt College and neighborhoods is a gentle wooded canyon that offers an opportunity to reconnect with nature. Leona Canyon Open Space Preserve, a 290-acre retreat located wholly within the city of Oakland.

Expect lots of dogs on the trail. If you bring your four-legged friend on this hike, just be sure to keep your dog out of the creek—otherwise use a leash. Leona Canyon isn't quite a "dog park," but a lot of hikers do bring their canine companions.

Don't expect any of the amenities (water, picnic areas, restrooms) common to other EBRPD units. Nearest restrooms are at Merritt College (when school is in session).

Leona Canyon Trail, the preserve's primary pathway, is a mellow, tree-shaded byway that travels through the canyon. Best vistas are from the northwest end of the trail near Merritt College.

From the depths of the canyon, two side trails—Artemesia Trail, ascending east and Pyrite Trail extending west offer short add-ons to the main hike. Out and back on Pyrite Trail will add about 1.5 miles to your canyon jaunt. That's the extent of the trail system; Anthony Chabot Regional Park is located just over the a hill and across Skyline Boulevard to the east, but you can't get there from here—at least by trail.

DIRECTIONS: From I-580 in Oakland, exit on Keller Avenue and drive east (toward the hills) 0.8 mile to Campus Drive. Turn left then make and almost immediate right on Canyon Oaks Drive. (The preserve is a little difficult to find since you have to drive into a condo complex in order to reach the parking lot.) Look for the signed trailhead, and at the end of Canyon Oaks, enter the Leona Canyon parking lot.

THE HIKE: From the gated fire road, descend wide Leona Canyon Trail. The path soon nears the creek at the mouth of the canyon then travels alongside Rifle Range Creek, part of the Arroyo Viejo Creek watershed. Just guessing there was once a rifle range here than inspired the name; before all those homes and condo-complexes were built nearby, this would have been the kind of secluded place ideal to do some shooting.

Travel a riparian corridor with a canopy of trees overhead—oak, bay, willow and alder. After a mild ascent, about 0.7 mile out, reach a signed junction with Artemesia Trail (that ascends slopes to the right and offers great vistas across the middle of the Bay).

Very soon thereafter, pass another signed junction with Pyrite Trail, which climbs west. Past these side trails, Leona Canyon Trail begins to climb out of the canyon. Near its end, the canyon levels and reaches a gate and a Merritt College parking lot. Kind of anticlimactic, but a good little hike.

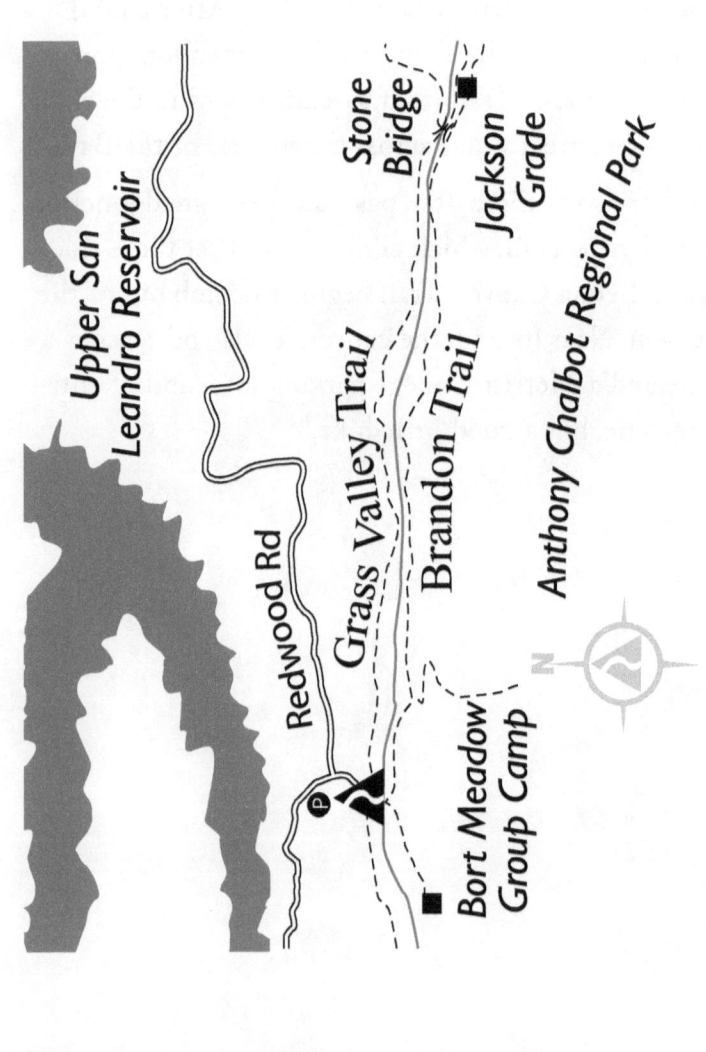

Anthony Chabot Regional Park

Grass Valley, Brandon Trails

3.4-mile loop

Sprawling across the hills above East Oakland and San Leandro, Anthony Chabot Regional Park beckons the hiker with miles and miles of trail that weave through eucalyptus groves, over chaparral-cloaked slopes and across sweeping grasslands. The 5,067-acre preserve is located adjacent to, and connected by trail with, popular Lake Chabot (Regional Park).

Out-of-towners tend to pronounce Chabot to rhyme with rabbit, a population of which bounds through the park's meadows. Canadian-born Anthony Chabot (rhymes with meadow and H_2O) was the hydraulic engineer and entrepreneur who developed Oakland's water system, as well as waterworks projects elsewhere around the Bay. Chabot created the lake that bears his name in 1874.

Redwoods were once a dominant feature here (and in neighboring Redwood Regional Park) but were all logged by the dawn of the 20th century. However, many second-growth trees are more than 100 years old now, and it's a pleasure to see them from the trail.

Chabot opened in 1952 as "Grass Valley Regional Park," originally named for what is the most notable natural feature in the northern part of the park. The long, grassy valley offers a most enjoyable hike. Grass Valley and Brandon trails offer a pleasant loop around the valley.

Want a longer loop (5.4 miles)? Take Grass Valley Trail to Stone Bridge (as described below), join the Jackson Grade connector, and loop back on Goldenrod Trail. Highlight is the spring wildflower display; downside is Goldenrod Trail's close proximity to Skyline Boulevard.

In 1874, water engineer Anthony Chabot created the lake that bears his name.

Anthony Chabot Regional Park

DIRECTIONS: From I-580 in Oakland, exit on Highway 13 and drive 4 miles. Exit on Redwood Road and proceed 5 miles to the trailhead (Bort Meadow Staging Area in Anthony Chabot Regional Park) on the right side of the road.

THE HIKE: From the parking area, descend paved Grass Valley Road. After 0.1 mile reach a three-way junction, look for Grass Valley Trail on the left, and join it.

(The road on the right goes to Bort Meadow, the trail in the middle connects to Brandon Trail, return route for this hike.)

Past the cattle gate, meander the nearly flat trail through narrow Grass Valley. About a mile out, pass a junction with Red Tail Trail and descend gently into a eucalyptus grove. At 1.7 miles, our hike halfway point, cross Stone Bridge (not surprisingly a stone bridge) and on on the other side of the creek meet Brandon Trail. (This path heads south to connect with Chabot's crazy-quilt of trails above the lake.)

Turn north on Brandon Trail and travel along the creek banks in the company of oak, bay, and the usual riparian vegetation mixed in with some handsome redwoods. A gentle ascent leads out of the creek corridor and back into the valley. As you close the loop, consider a short exploration/picnic around Bort Meadow, junction paved Grass Valley Road, and hoof it back up to the trailhead.

Ascend Rocky Ridge in Las Trampas Regional Wilderness: Definitely a hiker's park.

EVERY TRAIL TELLS A STORY.

II
Parks East and South

HIKE ON.

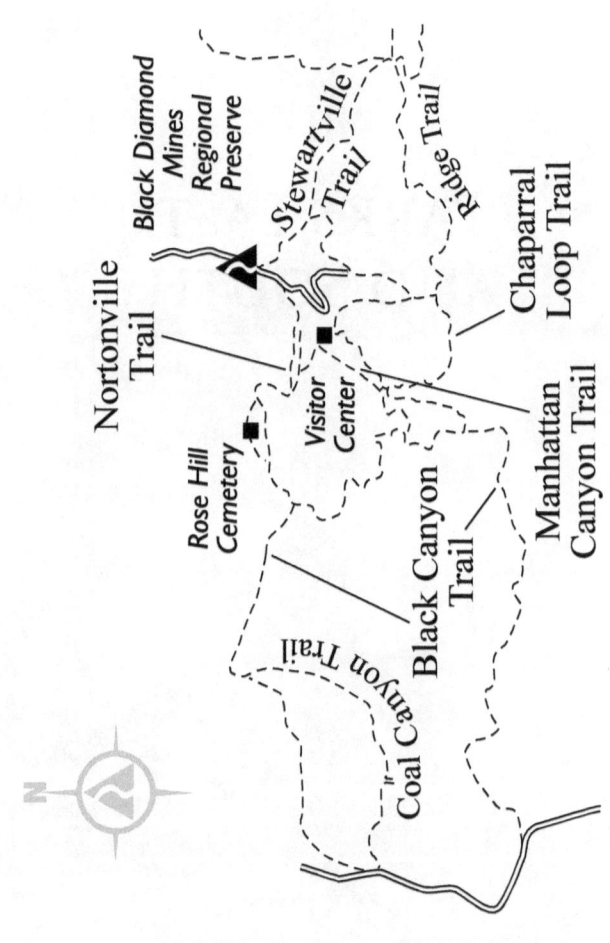

Black Diamond Mines Regional Park

Chaparral, Black Diamond, Coal Canyon, Nortonville Trails

5.2-mile loop with elevation gain

Everyone knows that West Virginia, not the East Bay, is coal mining country. Yet in the 1860s and 1870s the rugged hills east of Concord, known as the Mt. Diablo Coal Fields, yielded millions of tons of "black diamonds." The coal was shipped by rail to the coast at nearby Pittsburgh, and from there transported by boat to San Francisco or Stockton.

Extracting black diamonds was brutal work with pick and shovel, 12-hour days in cramped, dark, dusty confines of the mines. The miners dug more than 150 miles of tunnel through the hills. Gravestones in the cemetery testify that a miner's life was often a short one.

Despite hardships, towns such as Nortonville, Somersville, and Stewartsville were tidy places with shops and decent houses. Miners joined service clubs and fielded baseball teams renowned through the Bay area for their fine play.

By the mid 1880s, foreign imports and massive shipments of coal from fields in Oregon and Washington caused a precipitous decline in the local industry, which struggled until 1902 before finally ceasing. Millions of tons of coal are still believed to lie underground.

A second mining boom occurred in the 1920s when silica sand was extracted for use in local glassmaking industry. When this mining ended in 1949, the land remained abandoned, healing until the EBRPD acquired the land.

Today visitors can tour an underground mining museum and the Hazel-Atlas Mine, which supplied sand for a glassmaking company. Old mining roads, now park trails, wind past the sites of long-vanished mining towns.

The mountains here are not your basic rolling, rounded East Bay hills, but are more rugged, and resemble Gold Country Sierra foothills.

While there's an emphasis on mining history in this park, it's anything but the pits. More than 70 miles of trail travel grassy slopes that are dotted with blue oak, Coulter pine and gray pine. This hike loops through the heart of the park, passes two town sites and the Rose Hill Cemetery.

DIRECTIONS: From Highway 4 in Antioch, exit on Somersville Road. Drive south miles to Black Diamond Mines Regional Park. First parking lot is for the interpretive center, continue to road's end and the upper lot, where the trail begins

THE HIKE: At the visitor center, take the stairs to the right, and turn left. south to the Hazel-Atlas Mine and join the Chaparral Loop Trail. About 0.75 mile out, turn left on Manhattan Canyon Trail which dead-ends at the Black Diamond Trail at the 1-mile mark.

Turn left and begin a steady ascent into grasslands, gaining vistas of Martinez, San Francisco Bay and even the Marin Headlands. Just over 3 miles out, turn right (east) on Coal Canyon Trail and travel through a pine shaded canyon and the site of the Nortonville Mine.

Next comes a half-mile climb over the ridge of a hill to a cemetery. Pass through the cemetery and descend to the parking lot.

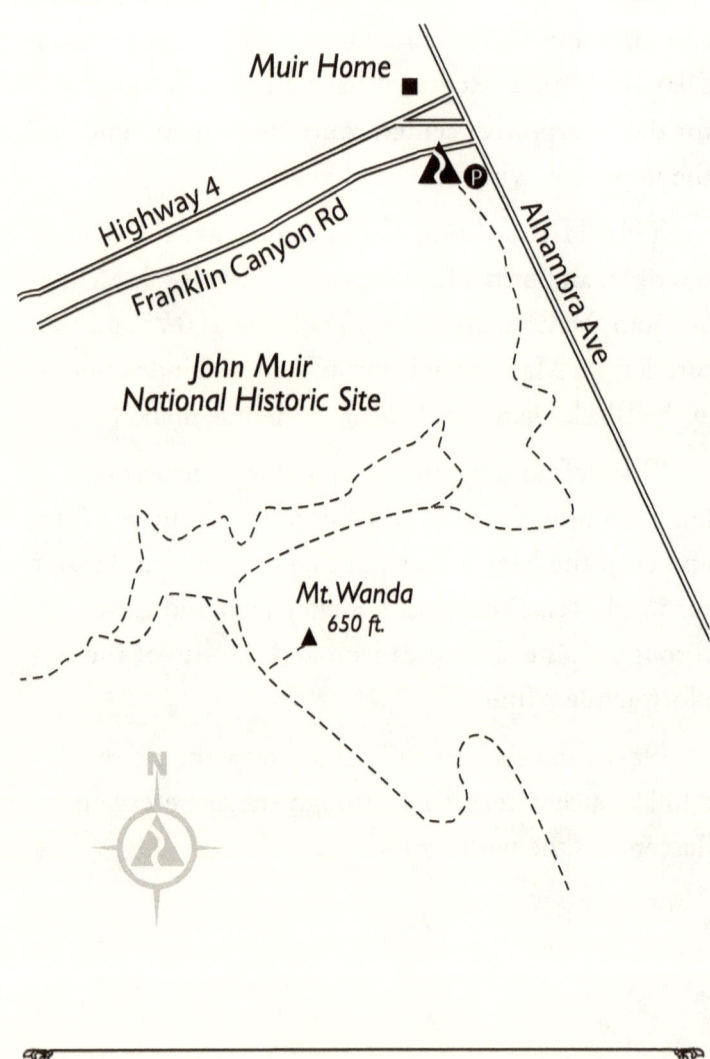

John Muir National Historic Site

John Muir Nature Trail

3-mile loop of Mt. Wanda with 400-foot elevation gain

At John Muir National Historic Site, tour the great naturalist's family home and take a hike in the rolling hills of his ranch, where he lived from 1890 until his death in 1914.

Most of us picture John Muir as a young man exploring the High Sierra and the wonders of Yosemite, or as America's revered elder naturalist, author and founder of the Sierra Club. We don't often think of Muir in his middle years—a time of great creativity and happiness for him, when he married, raised two daughters, and managed a fruit ranch on the outskirts of Martinez, California.

In 1880, Muir married Louie Strentzel, daughter of famed horticulturist Dr. John Strentzel. Muir proved to be a talented horticulturist himself and combined dedication to family and farm work with wilderness exploration and writing.

Allow an hour to an hour and a half to walk Orchard Trail and tour the Muir home, a handsome example of the upper middle-class Victorian lifestyle. Particularly intriguing are the parlors where the Muirs entertained and the Sierra Club Exhibit Room. Another highlight is John Muir's study (his "scribble den," as he called it) where he wrote magazine articles and books about America's wild lands.

(John Muir NHS is open Wednesday through Sunday, 10 a.m. to 4:30 p.m.)

The park includes 325 acres of rolling ranch land. High points, 660-foot Mt. Wanda and 640-foot Mt. Helen, are named after Muir's two daughters, who enjoyed walks in the hills with their father. John Muir Nature Trail, featuring Muir's advice to "break clear once in awhile and climb a mountain," along with a few fire roads, explore what's known as the "Mt. Wanda Area."

DIRECTIONS: From Highway 4 (John Muir Parkway), some 4 miles west of I-680, exit on Alhambra Avenue and drive north to John Muir National Historic Site. To hike Mt. Wanda, travel 0.25 mile south from the park visitor center on Alhambra Avenue to trailhead parking next to Franklin Avenue.

THE HIKE: Join the signed fire road and begin a steady climb above the John Muir Parkway and railroad trestles. As you climb, views open up to the east of mighty Mt. Diablo. To the north, view the town of Martinez, as well as the Carquinez Straits between San Pablo Bay and Suisun Bay.

About 0.75 mile from the trailhead, reach the signed beginning of the 1.3-mile long John Muir Nature Trail. The interpretive path delivers lessons about local geology, creeks, flora and fauna. Mt. Wanda natural highlights include a grand diversity of oaks—coast, live, valley, blue and black—and grassy meadows.

The nature trail ends at a junction with a fire road. Close the loop and return to the trailhead by turning left on the road. Other connecting fire roads allow you to extend your hike.

Muir home, circa 1900.

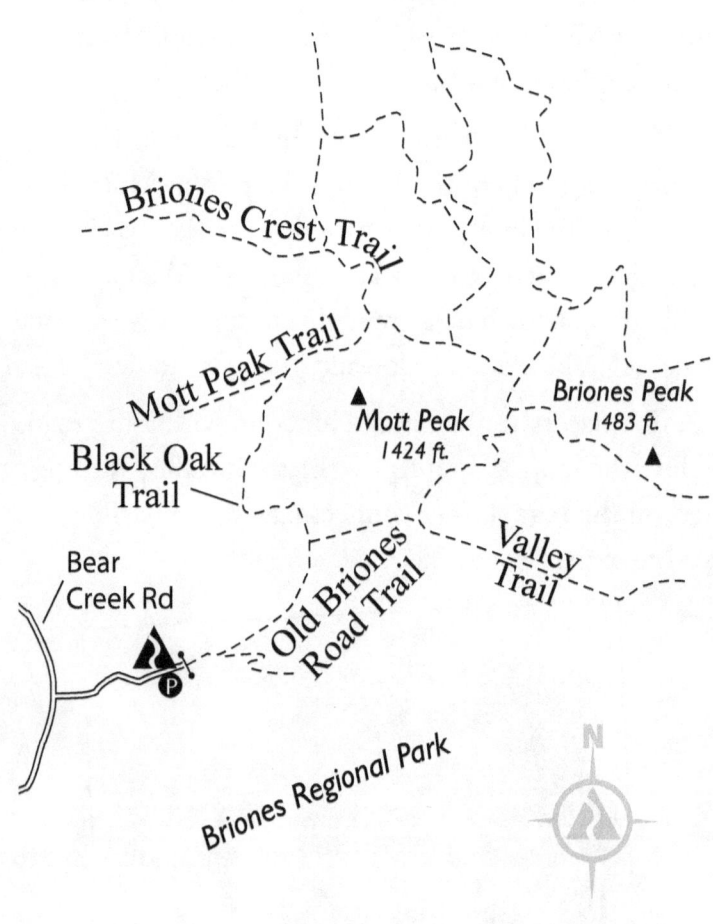

Briones Regional Park

Old Briones Road, Mott Peak, Black Oak Trails

4.4 miles round trip with 600-foot elevation gain

Located, indeed hidden, between popular Tilden Park and landmark Mt. Diablo, Briones Regional Park is easy to overlook. The park offers room to roam—6,117 acres of grassy hillsides.

Early Spanish settler Felipe Briones grazed cattle on his Rancho Felipe. The pastoral grasslands of the Bear Creek watershed were acquired by a water company in the early 1900s and by the East Bay Regional Park District in 1964.

The mostly undeveloped park offers the hiker pleasant excursions; several loops of varying lengths can be fashioned to explore the creeks and rolling hills. Include park high points, 1,424-foot Mott Peak and/or 1,483-foot Briones Peak in your hiking plans and you'll be rewarded with summit views of Mt.

Tamalpais to the west, Mt. Diablo the east, San Pablo and Suisun bays.

Trees partially obscure a portion of the view from Briones Peak; Mott Peak is treeless and a bit better positioned in the center of the park, so it offers slightly better 360-degree views.

This hike begins from the Bear Creek Meadows Trailhead in the southwest corner of the park and loops around Mott Peak. The peak honors William Penn Mott (1909-1992), EBRPD director, California State Parks director, founder of the California State Parks Foundation, and National Park Service director.

The park's grassy slopes are dotted with oaks and, in spring, with wildflowers—buttercups, lupine and fields of California poppies. Not that you could miss them, but the grasslands are dotted with cows, too!

DIRECTIONS: From I-580, exit on CA 24, drive 7 miles east and take the Moraga/Orinda exit. Turn left (north) and proceed 2 miles on Camino Pablo Road. Turn right on Bear Creek Road and follow it 4.5 miles to the park entry road (Briones Valley Road) on the right. Continue to road's end at the parking lot and trailhead.

THE HIKE: Join Old Briones Road (paved for its first 0.2 mile) and pass through a gate into cattle country. The path ascends parallel to a creek lined with oaks and California bay. About 0.75 mile out, pass Black Oak Trail (your return route) on the left, then ascend past a junction with Valley Trail.

About 1.7 miles out, reach a gate and a bench for resting and enjoy a panorama of the park and views of Mt. Diablo. Nearby is a junction with Briones Crest Trail; join this wide fire road and in 0.25 mile pass Lagoon Trail and "lagoons," ponds valuable to the resident birds and wildlife.

At the 2.4 mile-mark, meet Mott Peak Trail and join this fire road, which soon tops out and begins to descend the shoulder of Mott Peak. A spur trail leads to the peak.

After hiking just 0.36 mile on Mott Peak Trail, angle left (south) on Black Oak Trail. Down, up and down some more you go on this steep path that gets even steeper when it veers left (east) leading to a junction with Old Briones Road. Turn right and return to the trailhead.

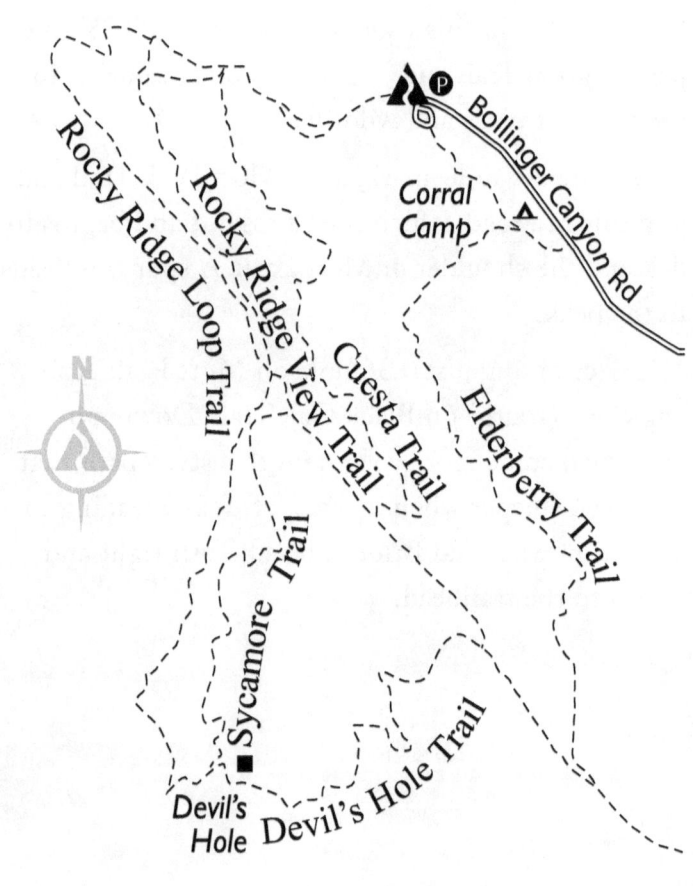

Las Trampas Regional Wilderness

Elderberry, Rocky Ridge View, Devil's Hole, Sycamore Trails

6.2-mile loop with 900-foot elevation gain

Las Trampas is definitely a "hiker's park," 5,342 acres of challenging terrain.

Las Trampas is Spanish for "The Traps." By some accounts, traps were set in these hills in order to snare elk. Another story has it that the Spanish observed the native Miwok driving elk and deer into narrow box canyon—"trapping" the animals for easier hunting.

Bisected by Bollinger Canyon, the park is comprised of two long hilly ridges. On the eastern side, Las Trampas Ridge is blanketed with chamise, sage, manzanita, and other chaparral plants. On the western side of the park lies Rocky Ridge, which features odd rock formations and wind caves, as well as mixed woodlands of bay laurel, buckeye, oak and big-leaf maple.

Some of the rocks on Rocky Ridge contain compressed layers of fossils. Millions of ancient seashells are embedded in the ridge. Fossil remains of a 3-toed horse, tusked mastodon—and even a rhinoceros have been discovered.

As for today's wildlife population, look for hawks, vultures, and the rare golden eagle soaring overhead, plus coyotes, opossums, and lots of rabbits. And domestic animals: cattle range the hills—grazing is allowed in order to keep the grass short (bovine-assisted fire prevention).

The climb up Rocky Ridge is a strenuous hike with a payoff: magnificent 360-degree views of Mt. Diablo. This hike is my favorite in the park, a 10K to remember, and a double butt-kicker: you climb the ridge twice!

Spring brings abundant wildflower displays, on the ridge, and especially in Sycamore Canyon. The EBRPD site offers a downloadable book that helps identify the many varieties.

The park's steep trails get very muddy after rains. Let things dry out a bit before you the trail.

DIRECTIONS: From I-680 in San Ramon, exit on Crow Canyon Road and drive 1 mile west to Bollinger Canyon Road. Turn right and drive 4 miles to the Las Trampas Regional Wilderness and to parking and the trailhead at road's end.

THE HIKE: Head through a cattle gate and southeast on Elderberry Trail for about 0.4 mile to Corral Camp (water and picnic tables). The path bends southwest and ascends steeply. About 1.7 miles from the camp, the trail ends at Rocky Ridge.

Make a hard right on Rocky Ridge View Trail and ascend another 0.3 mile to a 1,893 ridge high point and a junction with Devil's Hole Trail. Descend rapidly, losing 700 feet in elevation over the next 1.23 mile. Look for wind caves off the trail.

Just before reaching a creek crossing, spot Sycamore Trail on your right and join it. Up you go again! A steep ascent it is, a 1.25 mile climb over brushy slopes and past striking rock formations to meet Rocky Ridge Trail. Head left (north) for 0.75 mile then another 0.8 mile east on Rocky Ridge Trail back to the trailhead.

It's a short day's journey between Las Trampas and Eugene O'Neill parks; view Tao House along the way.

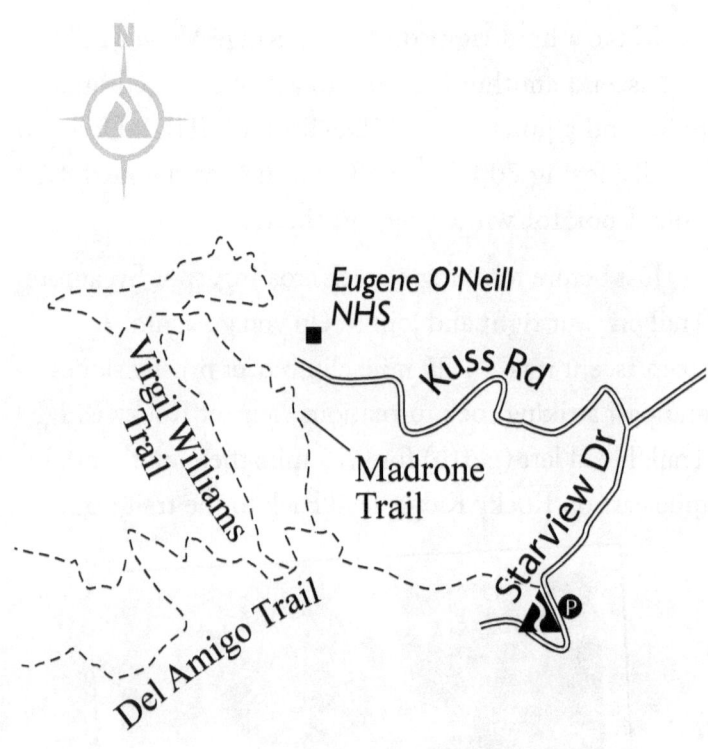

Eugene O'Neill National Historic Site

Del Amigo and Virgil Williams Trails

From Starview Drive to Eugene O'Neill NHS is 2 miles round trip with 400-foot elevation gain

When Eugene O'Neill, America's most distinguished playwright of the twentieth century, was awarded the Nobel Prize for literature in 1936 he used the prize money to build Tao House, his estate in the hills above Danville. In his seven years of residence in the hilltop retreat, O'Neill wrote his final plays, the often autobiographical masterworks "Long Day's Journey into Night," "The Iceman Cometh," and "A Moon for the Misbegotten."

You can tour the famed playwright's home and take a hike to it from adjacent Las Trampas Regional Wilderness. Visitors must have a reservation and nearly all visitors board a shuttle that departs from the Museum of the San Ramon Valley (205 Railroad

Ave in Danville). For more info, visit nps.gov/euon or call 925-838-0249 x6320. For hikers, a good time to visit is on Saturdays, when no reservations are required for self-guided tours. Figure about 1.5 hours for your visit and the National Park Service requests you arrive no later than 3 p.m.

Tao House reflects O'Neill's interest in Eastern thought and the passion of his wife, actress Carlotta Monterey, for Asian art and décor. The house is an unusual, even odd, blend of Spanish-California Mission architecture with Chinese style and design elements.

O'Neill's study is particularly intriguing to the many admirers of the playwright. His workplace, restored to near perfection with original and period furnishings, features a fireplace and private porch—a perfect place to write. Don't miss visiting the courtyard with its garden and pathways and a walk out to the swimming pool and nearby almond and walnut orchards.

A rare degenerative nerve disorder caused tremors in O'Neill's hands and he was literally unable to write; a creative shut-down followed and he never completed another play after 1943. The O'Neills moved to Boston where the great playwright died in 1953.

As you hike the beautiful hills and surrounding Tao House, you might conclude the beautiful East Bay scene was no inspiration for, and had no relation to, O'Neill's work. On the other hand, Tao House and surrounding natural beauty may have provided a setting conducive to reflection and the deep probing of the past that was so integral to his work.

DIRECTIONS: From Interstate 680 in Danville, exit on El Cerro Road and head west to Danville Boulevard. Turn right and go one block. Turn left on Del Amigo Road and follow it as it zigzags 0.5 mile to Starview Drive. Bear left and continue to the signed trailhead on the right side of the road. Park on Starview Drive (some restrictions posted) and not on the adjoining private road.

THE HIKE: Follow signed Del Amigo Trail along a fence line, soon leaving residences behind. Pass through a green gate and contour onto an open, lupine splashed slope with views out over Danville.

After about 0.6 mile you'll junction, then join, signed Virgil Williams Trail. You'll travel among ferns and old oaks that frame views of famed Mt. Diablo to the east.

The path dips to intersect Madrone Trail (a fire road). Turn right and cross a meadow, angling 0.2 mile toward a pond and the barn located in the back of Eugene O'Neill's home. A special visitor entrance is located on the side of Tao House.

Mission Peak

Hidden Valley, Eagle, Peak Trails

From Stanford Avenue Trailhead to summit is 6.2 miles round trip with 2,100-foot elevation gain

From a distance, it is the most austere of East Bay landmarks, a half-mile high hunk of mountain brooding over Silicon Valley. A nice place to go—if you're a mountain goat.

In closer view, Mission Peak is much more approachable and hiker-friendly than its steep west face suggests from afar. The summit is surrounded by Mission Peak Preserve, 3,000 acres of parkland that includes wooded canyons and gentle grassy hills grazed by cattle.

Oh my, Mission Peak a popular hike! On a busy weekend day, as many as two thousand hikers swarm the peak. Park officials suggest hikers consider alternate routes from Ohlone College or Ed R. Levin County Park.

Views from the 2,517-foot summit are well worth the considerable exertion—panoramas from San Jose to Mt. Tamalpais, Mt. Diablo to the Dunbarton Bridge. Perhaps only the hang gliders and turkey vultures circling Mission Peak have as good a view as the peak-conquering hiker.

The peak takes its name from Mission San Jose, founded in 1797. The climb up Mission Peak is quite simply one of those classic Bay Area hikes that belongs on every local hiker's, and every traveling hiker's, "To Do" list.

Best days to do it are cool, clear ones. Summer, with its thick, view-obscuring, morning fog and hot, hiker-toasting, afternoon sun is the worst time to hike Mission Peak. Autumn and winter are excellent times, when the clearest of days mean vistas for hikers from the Santa Cruz Mountains to the High Sierra.

DIRECTIONS: From Highway 680 in Fremont, exit on Mission Boulevard and head north 0.25 mile. Turn right on Stanford Avenue and proceed 0.6 mile to road's end at a parking area.

THE HIKE: Walk up the major dirt road (Hidden Valley Trail). To the right (east) of the trail is Peak Meadow Trail, which leads to Horse Heaven Trail; the two paths offers an alternative way up (or down) Mission Peak.

Cross Agua Caliente Creek and begin a robust ascent over grassy slopes punctuated by coast live oaks along the way. As the din of the city fades away, pass another junction with Peak Meadow Trail and climb farther into cattle country. Personally I've found the cows to be contented; other hikers report aggressive behavior.

The going gets rockier and, just as you start to think the trail is taking you away from rather than toward the peak, you reach a three-way junction at the 2.3 mile mark. Bear right (on Eagle Trail), and bend right (northeast).

Nearing the summit, the trail levels briefly. Bear right on Peak Trail, then climb steeply on the narrow path past rock outcroppings to the summit. Up top is the curious "Mission Peeker," sighting tubes aimed at natural landmarks as well as a now iconic monument, a sculpture/time capsule that promotes environmental awareness and top tourist attraction.

Patience atop Mission Peak: Wait your turn to take a selfie at the summit.

Sunol Regional Wilderness

Indian Joe, Canyon View Trails

From Visitor Center to Little Yosemite is a 3.5-mile loop with 300-foot elevation gain; or 5.5-mile loop with a 500-foot gain.

If you have Yosemite National Park firmly in mind it's a stretch to call this isolated canyon east of Fremont "Little Yosemite." The small waterfalls don't resemble Vernal Falls or Yosemite Falls and the canyon's rock outcroppings don't call to mind Half Dome or Cathedral Rocks.

On the other hand, Little Yosemite doesn't require shuttle buses, reservations, a long trip and contending with crowds. The East Bay's Little Yosemite, a narrow gorge cut by Alameda Creek, offers boulders, cascades, and more, just a short hike from the park's visitor center.

Alameda Creek flows through the southern part of Sunol Regional Wilderness, a 6,850-acre preserve of rolling, grassy hills dotted with oak and madrone. The preserve seems a perfect pastureland of pastoral hills and valleys, though with all the cows grazing here you have to wonder about the "wilderness" in the park name.

Hikers enjoy lots of room to roam, one grassy hill after another, the pattern interrupted only by occasional rock outcroppings and oak groves. From highpoints whose very names suggest they offer good views—Eagle's View, Vista Grande, Flag Hill—you can gaze out at even more backcountry belonging to EBRPD.

There are many ways to tour the park and reach Little Yosemite. For a longer loop, ascend grassy slopes along the sycamore- and oak-lined Indian Joe Creek. A mile out, you'll reach Cave Rocks, a basalt-schist conglomerate popular with rock-climbers and picnickers. After another 0.25 mile of climbing you'll near the ridgetop and bear right on Cave Rocks Road. Enjoy the expansive views from the open ridge as you descend to Cerro Este Overlook and Road, and continue on a southern descent to Camp Ohlone Road, then over the Little Yosemite area.

First-time Sunol sojourners will appreciate Canyon View Trail, which offers the most direct route to Little Yosemite. (Note: swimming is not permitted.) Drop by Old Green Barn Visitor Center for info about self-guided Indian Joe Nature Trail and interpretive programs.

DIRECTIONS: From I-680, just south of the community of Sunol, exit on Calaveras Road. Head south 5 miles to Geary Road. Turn left and follow this road to its end and the park entrance. The hiking begins by the park's small visitor center.

THE HIKE: From the visitor center, cross a wooden bridge spanning Alameda Creek and follow signs for Indian Joe Nature Trail. After 0.25 mile, join Canyon View Trail, a narrow footpath, pass through a cattle gate, and ascend the canyon walls for vistas of the steep canyon.

Reach a junction with McCorkle Trail (a mile-long length of this trail and another mile on Cerro Este Road offers a worthy extension to this hike). Canyon View Trail levels a bit and descends to Cerro Este Road, which you follow another 0.2 mile to Camp Ohlone Road and Little Yosemite. Return via Ohlone Road or Canyon View Trail.

Yosemite in miniature? Some hikers think so.

Mt. Diablo Summit
The Grand Loop

7 miles round trip with 500-foot elevation gain

From the Golden Gate to the Farallon Islands, and from the High Sierra to the Central Valley—this is the sweeping panorama you can savor from atop Mt. Diablo. Impressive, considering the mountain's relatively short height (3,849 feet). Two reasons for the grand views: 1) the mountain rises solo very abruptly from its surroundings 2) the land surrounding the mountain—the San Franciso Bay and Central Valley—is nearly flat.

In 1931, the upper slopes of Mt. Diablo were preserved as a state park. In more recent years, the lower slopes were added to the park (which now totals 20,000 acres), thanks in a large measure to the efforts of Save Mt. Diablo, a local conservation organization.

A great way to tour the mountain is to follow what park rangers call "The Grand Loop," a seven-mile circuit that connects several trails and fire roads and offers views of—and from—Diablo in every direction.

Mt. Diablo boasts some fine trails but even the most ardent hiker will admit the state park seems to have been designed for the automobile. Still, there are plenty of places on Diablo's flanks where cars can't go, as we shall soon see.

DIRECTIONS: From Interstate 680 northbound from the Pleasanton / Dublin area, exit on Diablo Blvd in Danville traveling to the east. Diablo Road makes several turns en route to Mt. Diablo Scenic Drive. Continue on Diablo Road past a fire station on the right until you reach Mt. Diablo Scenic Drive. Turn left and follow this road into the park. To reach the summit, turn right on Summit Road at the Junction Ranger office.

THE HIKE: After partaking of the view, join Summit Trail, descending from the southeast side of the lower lot and in 0.25 mile meet North Peak Trail, also located by the paved road.

Summit Trail heads southwest down the mountain, but you join the eastward-trending trail to North Peak. Enjoy the awesome view of the Central Valley as you march over a rocky, juniper-dotted slope. The red-brown rock formation above looks more than a little diabolical; the most prominent rock formation is known as Devil's Pulpit.

North Peak Trail descends to a distinct saddle, Prospector's Gap, and a four-way junction, 1.4 miles from the trailhead. Take signed Prospector's Gap Fire Road west to an intersection with northbound Donner Creek Fire Road, whereupon the route continues west as Meridian Ridge Fire Road.

Past a junction with Eagle Peak Trail, the fire road bends south and crosses Deer Flat Creek and reaches Deer Flat, a pleasant rest stop shaded by blue oak, located at about the four-mile mark of this hike. Begin a moderately steep, mile-long ascent to reach Deer Flat Road and bear left, southeast, savoring the views and (in springtime) wildflowers.

Another mile of hiking brings you to Juniper Picnic Area and Campground. From the campground, join Juniper Trail, which climbs a ridge to reach Summit Road and short path leading to the lower parking lot.

Sharp focus: Mt. Diablo offers expansive views of the East Bay—and far beyond.

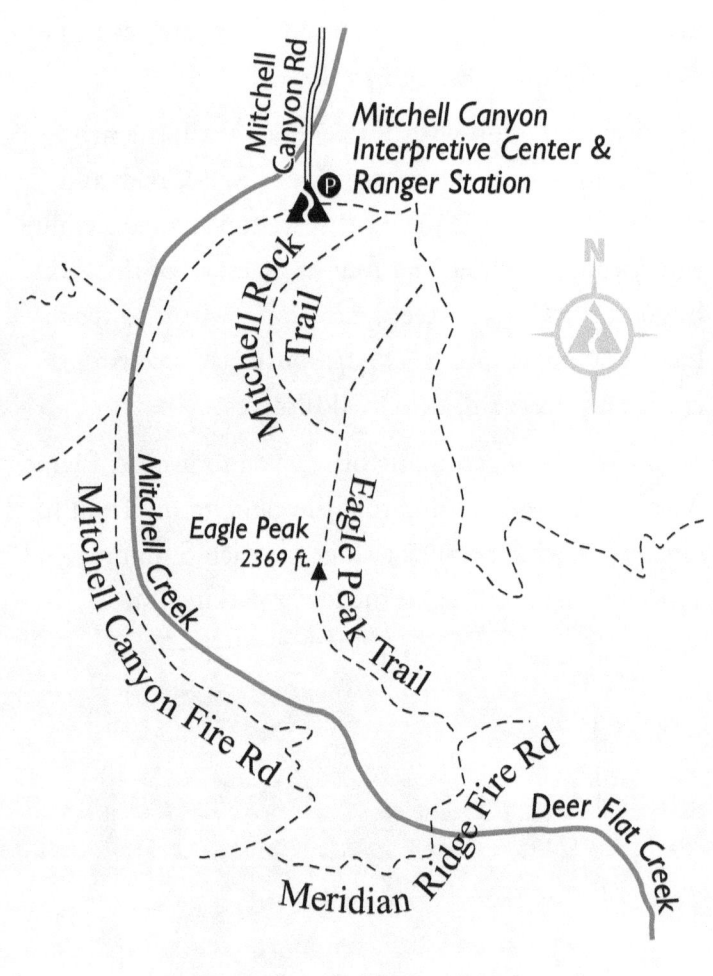

TheTrailmaster.com

Mitchell Canyon & Eagle Peak

Mitchell Canyon, Meridian Ridge, Eagle Peak, Mitchell Rocks Trails

8-mile loop with 1,800-foot elevation gain

Along with its unrivalled summit panoramas, from the Golden Gate Bridge to the High Sierra, the mighty mountain also has a more subtle appeal to the senses, a quiet beauty that brings hikers back to Diablo again and again to explore the state park. Botanists say Mt. Diablo's slopes support one of the Bay Area's greatest numbers of flowering plants.

In springtime, meadows blossom with buttercups, blue-eyed grass and blue dicks. Other common blooms include Indian paintbrush, clarkia, larkspur and California fuchsia. The keen-eyed wildflower lover might even spot the rare Mt. Diablo globe lily, a squat yellow flower with a blossom shaped like a small lantern; it grows only on and around the mountain.

Mitchell Canyon trailhead is departure point for long loops around the park and for the grueling (14-miles round trip with 3,200-foot elevation gain) hike to Diablo's summit, definitely one of the East Bay's most challenging days on the trail. The trailhead offers restrooms, visitor center, picnic tables and large parking lot.

The loop hike through Mitchell Canyon and over Eagle Peak is a particular favorite of mine because it's such a fine tour of Mt. Diablo's diverse ecology—grasslands, oak savannas, chaparral slopes, riparian communities and more. Diablo's shoulders boast a multitude of trees: alder and big-leaf maple along Mitchell Creek, beautiful drifts of blue oak and live oak, gray pine perched on the upper slopes.

DIRECTIONS: From Interstate 680 in Walnut Creek, exit on Ygnacio Road. Drive east 7.5 miles to Clayton Road. Turn right (south) and proceed a mile to Mitchell Canyon Road. Turn right and continue 1.5 miles until road's end at the state park's day-use parking area.

THE HIKE: Mitchell Canyon Fire Road is a nature trail for the first two miles of its length; pick up a nature guide at the trailhead. Soon pass the Mitchell Rock Trail (your return route) on the left, and pass junctions with right-forking Black Point Trail 0.6 mile out, and Red Road at 0.9. As the canyon widens, you can see rocky Eagle Peak.

Two miles out, the trail steepens, leaves the cool creekside environs and heads onto drier slopes cloaked with chaparral. Reach a couple of picnic tables and soon thereafter Deer Flat Junction at 3.5 miles.

Continue left on Meridian Ridge Road, descend briefly, then climb again to Murchio Gap at 4.2 miles and a five-way junction. Turn left onto narrow rocky Eagle Peak Trail, which descends then climbs again to the top of Eagle Peak (a narrow ridgeline). Enjoy the view of the summit of Diablo and North Peak then descend chaparral slopes. At the 6-mile mark Eagle Peak Trail bends right. Continue straight with Mitchell Rock Trail. Look left for Mitchell Rock, a basalt outcropping. At the junction with Mitchell Canyon Fire Road, turn right and return to the trailhead.

Take a hike on Bay Trail, which leads through Hayward Regional Shoreline and all around the East Bay.

EVERY TRAIL TELLS A STORY.

III
BY THE BAY

HIKE ON.

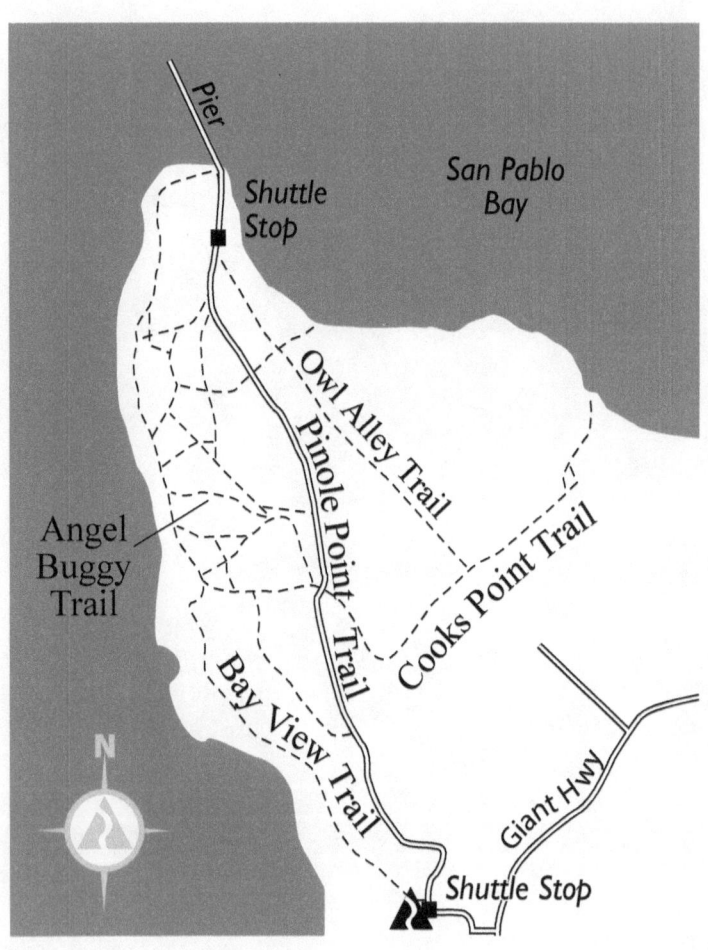

Point Pinole Regional Shoreline
Bay View Trail

To Point Pinole Pier is 3.6 miles round trip

This park started out with a bang. For nearly 100 years, Atlas Powder Company and other firms made gunpowder and dynamite at Point Pinole. The explosives industry relocated to the then-remote locale from San Francisco after a series of unfortunate events and accidental blasts. Manufacturing ceased in 1960, and Point Pinole Regional Shoreline opened to the public in 1973.

The former factory site makes for an unusual park. Eucalyptus, planted with the intention of the trees blocking the sight and sound of any unplanned explosions, now offer habitat for deer, birds and migrating Monarch butterflies. Service roads are now part of a network of recreation trails.

The park's 2,315 acres includes meadows, marshland, bay shore, a freshwater pond and eucalyptus woodland. This diversity of habitats and the park's location on the Pacific Flyway attracts more than 100 species of birds—scads of shorebirds and ducks, plus herons, egrets and red-winged blackbirds. Look high in the sky for red-tailed hawks and vultures.

Longtime East Bay landmark Point Pinole is positioned where the shoreline bends from its north-south orientation along Berkeley and Oakland to the east (inland). From the point, get great views across San Pablo Bay to the cities and hills to the north and east; to Marin and Mt. Tam to the northwest; to San Francisco to the southwest.

Don't miss the walk onto Point Pinole's 1,250-foot fishing pier, which offers picnic tables, great fishing and fabulous views. Quickest way to the Point and pier is via paved 1.5-mile long Point Pinole Road. Even quicker and easier: a low-cost shuttle service transports visitors from parking lot to pier.

For hikers, the most compelling path to the pier is Bay View Trail (a segment of San Francisco Bay Trail). The path serves up views and links to numerous trails that lead to the shore and marshlands.

DIRECTIONS: From I-80 on the northern edges of Richmond, exit on Richmond Parkway, drive west 2 miles, and exit on Giant Highway. Turn right and follow the signs another mile to the park entry on your left.

THE HIKE: Walk north on paved Point Pinole Road, cross a bridge over the train tracks and, 0.2 mile from the start, join signed Bay View Trail, a gravel path. Head shoreward, then walk along the bay. Benches offer westward views over the bay and beach access trails lead to water's edge.

Pass through eucalyptus woodland, reach the mile-mark and, in the next 0.25 mile, pass a flurry of footpaths: Biazzi, Nitro, Angel Buggy, Packhouse trails. It's easy to stay on Bay View Trail—just follow the signs and keep the bay on your left!

About 1.6 mile out, the trail crosses a grassland, bay views get even better. Descend Bay View Trail to the paved road near the pier.

After enjoying a walk on the pier, return the same way, via Point Pinole Road, or improvise a route (suggestion: Owl Alley and Cook's Point Trail) back to the trailhead.

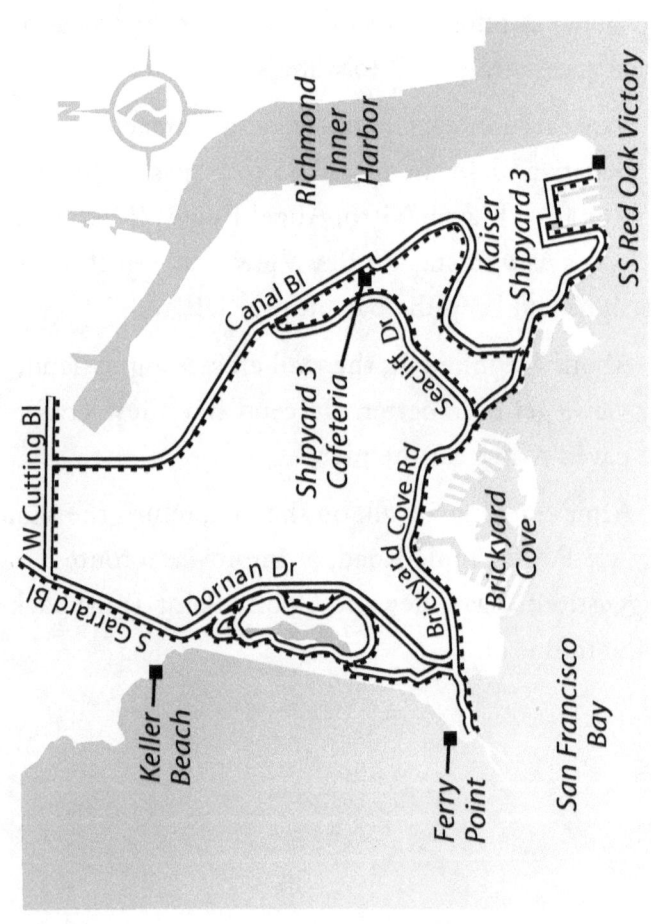

Miller Knox Regional Shoreline

Ferry Point Loop Trail

3.6 miles round trip

Enjoy a picnic or swim in San Francisco Bay in this 306-acre park that offers the urban hiker a few intriguing ways to go. A mile-long paved trail loops around a saltwater marsh lagoon, habitat for abundant waterfowl.

Ferry Point Loop Trail, a 3.6-mile length of the San Francisco Bay Trail, circles the park. The path connects with Kaiser Shipyard 3 Trail that leads to Rosie the Riveter WW II Home Front National Historical Park. Completed in 2015, the new trail is garnering great reviews; some hikers regard it as one of the most scenic and historic stretches of the Bay Trail.

Ferry Point Loop Trail is a grand tour of a 20th century industrial shoreline, beginning in 1900 when the Santa Fe Railroad tunneled through the Portola Hills and extended its tracks to Richmond Point aka Ferry Point.

In 1907 the Richmond Pressed Brick Company began making bricks—shipping them to San Francisco, then undergoing a massive rebuilding effort after the devastating 1906 earthquake.

The opening of the Panama Canal in 1915 spurred Richmondites to position their city and waterfront as a player in world trade. A wharf was built and a ferry service launched between Richmond and San Rafael. In 1942, just after America's entry into World War II, four shipyards were constructed on the Richmond waterfront. Kaiser Shipyard 3 is the only one remaining. The *S.S. Red Oak Victory*, the only ship built in Richmond not scrapped, is docked in the port where it was built and is today a museum ship.

The East Bay Regional Park District opened the Miller-Knox Regional Shoreline in 1970, and in 2000 Rosie the Riveter WW II Home Front National Historical Park was created.

DIRECTIONS: From I-580 in Richmond, exit on Canal Boulevard. Turn left onto Canal Boulevard, right onto W. Cutting Boulevard, the left onto S. Garrard Boulevard. Proceed through the tunnel (S. Garrard Boulevard continues as Dornan Drive) for 0.5 mile. Turn right into the main park entrance or drive another 0.25 mile to the Ferry Point entrance.

THE HIKE: It's a short walk to Ferry Point, where there are picturesque ruins of the old ferry landing and excellent bay views. Join signed Bay

Trail, which leads alongside Brickyard Cove Road and past the Richmond Yacht Club. In front of the large Brickyard Landing condominium complex stand a tall brick smokestack and two beehive-shaped kilns, reminders of the brick-making operations that manufactured "Richmond red" bricks.

Bay Trail bends northeast and ascends alongside Seacliff Drive. (For a fun side trip, ascend the dirt pathway that climbs north to East Vista Point and affords fine views of the bay, Angel Island, and Alcatraz Island.) The trail then descends, offers a commanding view of Richmond's industrial shoreline, and leads to Canal Boulevard, about 1.5 miles from Ferry Point.

The next mile of walking is not very interesting, but keep the faith; the last leg of Ferry Point Loop Trail is lots more intriguing. Go left alongside Canal Boulevard and in 0.6 mile, go left again on W. Cutting Boulevard. After 0.25 mile, turn left on South Garrard.

At West Richmond Avenue, find pubs and eateries. Pass by the impressive Richmond Municipal Natatorium, commonly known as The Plunge, built in 1926, and wonderfully restored. The trail leads through the Ferry Point Tunnel and emerges near Keller Beach and the main part of Miller-Knox Regional Park.

Take the path that extends along the west side of the lagoon and past picnic grounds. Keep walking along the park shoreline; paved and gravel pathways lead back to Dornan Drive and the Ferry Point entry where you began the hike.

Real-life Rosie the Riveters celebrate at a reunion held at the historical park.

Rosie the Riveter WW II Home Front National Historical Park

Shipyard 3 Trail

From Shipyard 3 Cafeteria to Kaiser Shipyard 3 is 3 miles round trip

Only the National Park Service could create a historical park to tell the story of World War II on the homefront—and the vital contribution of women to the war effort. And it is altogether fitting that Richmond is the site of Rosie the Riveter WW II Home Front National Historical Park.

The war years were a time of massive relocation for Americans as they moved in unprecedented numbers around the country to take war jobs. Six million women, symbolized by the iconic Rosie the Riveter image, entered the workforce. The population of the city of Richmond swelled from 24,000 to 100,000 and the factories operated 24 hours a day to build ships, Jeeps and tanks.

The socioeconomic and cultural effects of this explosive growth were significant. Men and women of different races and backgrounds lived together, worked together, in close proximity.

Best place to begin your exploration of the park and its scattered historical sites is at the excellent park visitor center, which offers interpretive programs, films, interactive exhibits, and gift store.

To war planners tasked with building ships and building them fast, Richmond had much to offer: a deep water port, plenty of waterfront, and a rail line already in place. During the war years, the Kaiser Shipyards produced 747 ships, making them the most productive shipyards in history.

A segment of the Bay Trail, Shipyard 3 Trail is a fine add-on to the Ferry Point Loop or a worthwhile excursion on its own. Interpretive panels tell the story of the war effort—of which much evidence remains in the form of docks, railway line, buildings, as well as an enormous crane and even a ship. About that ship: the *S.S. Red Oak Victory* is the only Richmond-built vessel surviving from the era. Now a museum, it's back in the dock where it was built. Kaiser Shipyard 3 was built to last—beyond the war years—and that's a key reason, historians say, that so much of the shipyard is still intact after all these years.

DIRECTIONS: From I-580 West, take the Harbour Way South exit. Turn right onto Cutting Blvd. Make a right on Harbour Way South, continue 0.8 miles. Check-in at a security post just before the large Ford assembly building. Drive behind the Ford building to the visitor center located in a smaller brick building near the water.

The trailhead for Shipyard Trail is 3.3 miles away via Harbour Way South and Canal Boulevard.

THE HIKE: From the Shipyard 3 cafeteria building (circa 1943), join the signed Shipyard Trail. After 0.2 mile, take the dirt path that switchbacks up to a vista point and interpretive panels that tell of the shipyard and the "Dynamic Wartime Port." Continue along the industrial shoreline and past newly built waterfront flats and townhomes.

After 1.2 miles, the trail curves southeast along the waterfront and approaches the shipyard. Walk past the docks and warehouses over to the *S.S. Red Oak Victory*. Don't miss—maybe you can't miss—the giant Whirley Crane. Workers, some of them women, sat high in the turret atop the crane that hoisted massive prefabricated sheets of iron into place to construct the ships.

Love that trail logo: Rosie the Riveter lives on.

A tour to remember: Paddle across the Bay to Brooks Island and take a hike.

Brooks Island

Ever wondered about that island that lies just beyond Richmond Harbor?

It's Brooks Island, a 373-acre preserve, a sanctuary for birds, and perhaps the East Bay's most obscure hiking destination.

You can visit Brooks Island Regional Preserve only by joining an East Bay Regional Park District tour (more info and costs: EBParks.org, 888-327-2757). The tour includes a short paddle in a kayak across the bay to the island and along the isle's shoreline, plus a two-mile long, naturalist-led hike.

The tour is educational in the best sense of the word. It's packed with colorful tales of the island's unusual history and gives you the chance to learn first-hand about this special environment.

Brooks Island has a long and colorful history. Archaeologists estimate the native Ohlone first lived on the island some 3,000 years ago. The size of several shellmounds on the isle suggest a prolonged period of occupation by the Ohlone.

During the 19th century, the island was used to graze sheep and known as Sheep Island. And when it was used as a quarry (1892-1938), it was sometimes known as Rocky Island. As the story goes, sandstone from the island quarry was used by prisoners to build a cell block on San Quentin in 1913, and in later years to construct foundations for Treasure Island and the Bay Bridge toll plaza.

During the 1960s, the Sheep Island Gun Club populated the isle with quail, pheasants and other birds for club members (which included singer Frank Sinatra) to shoot. The East Bay Regional Park District acquired the island in 1968. The agency has more or less administered Brooks Island as a nature preserve ever since.

Human disturbance of the isle's ecology has been relatively modest, and nature is on full display. For botanists and native plant fans, the island is renowned for its coastal grassland. Native purple needle grass and ryegrass thrive here and have not been overwhelmed by the various nonnative species as they have elsewhere around the Bay Area.

Wildlife on the island includes garter snakes, salamanders and the Pacific tree frog. Harbor seals haul-out on island shores en route from their rookery on Castro Rocks.

By far the most commonly sighted animal is the California vole, aka the California meadow mouse.

The voles arrived on the island as a result of science experiment gone wrong. In 1957, scientists introduced 7 voles (3 females, 4 males) onto nearby Bird Island with the intention of measuring their reproduction rate in an isolated habitat. Turns out voles are excellent swimmers (*Who knew?*) and they swam over to Brooks Island, a kind of Vole Heaven for the six-inch long herbivorous creatures, given that their favorite food source is wild grasses. Judging by the sheer number of burrows that pockmark the grasslands, the voles continue to reproduce at a rapid rate.

The island's tidal flats and salt marshes are habitat for many species of birds, including nesting herons and egrets. Among birders, Brooks is best known for the bay's largest nesting colony of Caspian terns, which occupy a two mile long manmade sandspit that extends west from the north side of the island. Just off the southwest coast of the island lies tiny Bird Island, a nesting site for Canada geese, black oystercatchers, and Western gulls.

Put a visit to Brooks Island on your bucket list: an island adventure, right here in the East Bay!

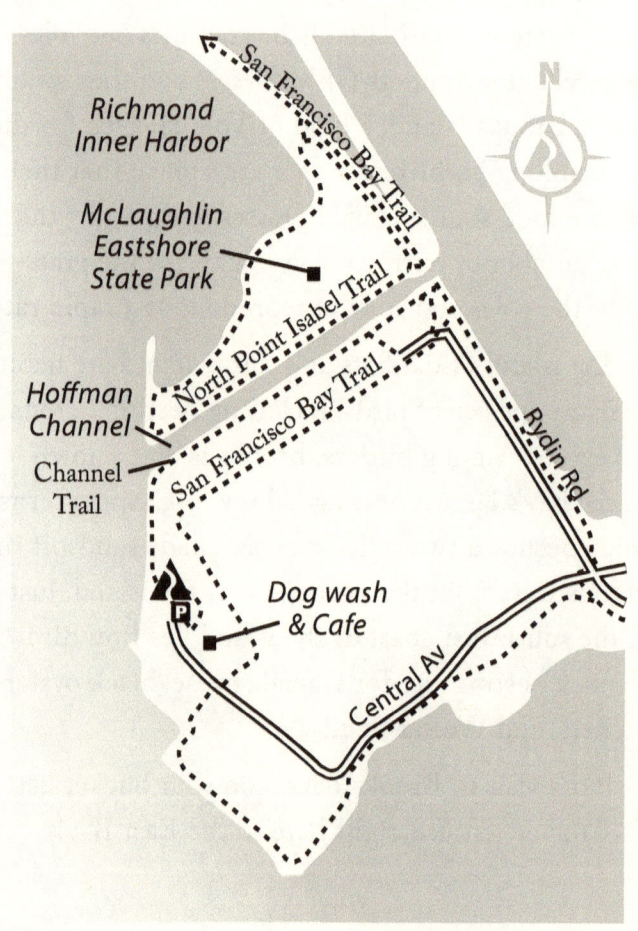

McGlaughlin Eastshore State Park

Bay Trail

From Point Isabel to Shimada Friendship Park is 3.4 miles round trip

Explore 8.5 miles of San Francisco's East Bay shoreline from the Oakland Bay Bridge to Richmond in a park located amidst one of the state's mostly highly urbanized areas.

Renamed in 2012 to honor Save the Bay co-founder Sylvia McLaughlin, Eastshore State Park is an interesting combination of natural wetlands, and mudflats, restored wetlands, and upland created by fill placement in the bay west of the original shoreline. When you walk this shore, you take in hugely contrasting sights and sounds: the sight of bush lupine blowing in the breeze by the bay and the enormous U.S. Postal Service bulk mail facility oh-so-close to Point Isabel; the sound of bird songs along the Bay Trail and the roar of traffic along I-580.

An outstanding example of open space preservation, about half the park is managed for wildlife and conservation purposes and the balance oriented to recreation. Hiking, bicycling and bird-watching are among the most popular activities in the park. Pedestrian and cycling pathways extend throughout Eastshore State Park.

When created in 2002, Eastshore State Park represented the culmination of a 20-year effort for local conservationists and array of government officials. Jointly managed by California State Parks and the East Bay Regional Parks District, the park includes both upland and tideland along the waterfronts of Richmond, Albany, Berkeley, Emeryville and Oakland.

Point Isabel Regional Park is sort of a park within a park. Make that a dog park. The park allows, even encourages, dogs. While their human companions enjoy vistas across the bay to Angel Island and San Francisco, dogs can roam free and off-leash. The park is extremely popular, attracting nearly 1.5 million visitors a year and who knows how many dogs.

Often called the "Point Isabel Dog Park," its maintained and kept pretty darn clean by the Point Isabel Dog Owners (PIDO). Dog-owners can get a bite at the Sit & Stay Café while their dogs get groomed just steps away at Mudpuppy's Tub & Scrub.

This hike offers a choice of flat, dirt and paved routes. Pathways loop around Point Isabel. The Point is bisected by Hoffman Channel, and you can circle both halves—Point Isabel proper and North Point Isabel—using loop trails and the footbridge between them.

You can also choose to walk the Bay Trail north toward Richmond. (Dogs must be on leash.) For a fine 3.4-mile outing, walk from Point Isabel to Shimada Friendship Park, named for Richmond's sister city, which offers picnic facilities, and an excellent place for sunset watching.

DIRECTIONS: From I-580 or I-80 (the Eastshore Freeway) in Richmond, exit on Central Avenue and head west then north to reach the Point Isabel Regional Shoreline parking lots.

THE HIKE: From the west end of the parking lot, join dog-walkers on the trails along Hoffman Channel and check out the many species of birds (and dogs!). Cross the bridge over Hoffman Channel and wander the trails of North Point Isabel or just walk north on Bay Trail, which follows the route of railroad line, built in 1968 but never used.

Observe nature on both sides of the levy in the form of abundant bird life plus native flora such as lizardtail, monkeyflower and sagebrush, as well as plenty of interpretive panels to tell you all about the natural world.

Enjoy great views to the west and south and across Richmond Harbor to Brooks Island (see description). Shimada Friendship Park is a good turnaround point, though the intrepid can continue many more miles on Bay Trail.

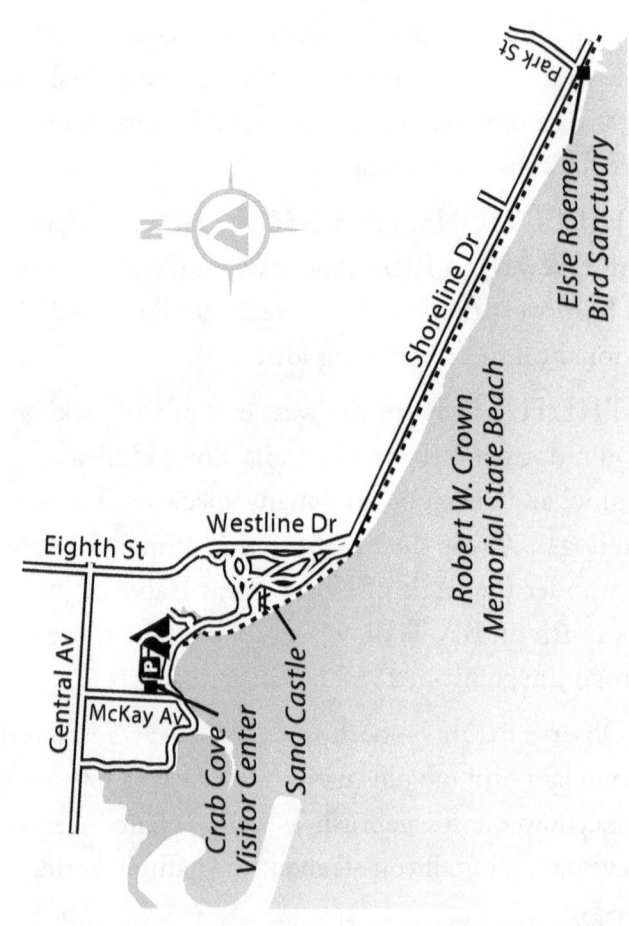

CROWN BEACH
CROWN BEACH TRAIL

From Crab Cove Visitor Center to Elsie Roemer Bird Sanctuary is 5 miles round trip

Located in the city of Alameda, Crown Memorial State Beach is known for its warm waters for swimming, inviting picnic grounds, kayaking, sail-boarding and its bike path. Hikers can enjoy the more natural features of the park—sand dunes, bird sanctuary, a marine reserve—on a leisurely walk along the 2.5-mile long beach.

Alameda Beach, as it was once known, was the largest beach on San Francisco Bay and quite the amusement center (the "Coney Island of the West") from the 1880s through the 1930s. Carnivals, concerts, baseball games, hot-air balloon rides, boxing matches attracted Bay Area residents to this shore.

By the 1970s the beach was in danger of eroding away by a combination of wind and waves. In the 1980s, sand from San Francisco Bay was pumped by a barge and sent ashore via a pipeline. More engineering kept the sand in place, and then the uplands got a landscaping makeover.

Improvements continued over the years, creating the attractive parkland visitors enjoy today. The most natural areas are Crab Cove, a nature reserve located at the north end of the park and Elsie Roemer Bird Sanctuary at the east end.

Learn more about the colorful history of this beach at the park's Crab Cove Visitor Center. Exhibits and an aquarium highlight the ecology of the San Francisco Bay.

Operated by the East Bay Regional Park District, the beach honors the late State Assemblyman Robert W. Crown, who worked to preserve this coastline as parkland. The park is known for its free concerts and annual Sand Castle and Sand Sculpture Contest, held in front of the bathhouse on a low tide Saturday morning in June. Many park facilities are accessible to wheelchair users and beach wheelchairs, intended to provide a means for wheelchair users to travel across the beach, are available free of charge.

Beach walking is best at low tide, and low tides are the best for observing shorebirds that live along the mudflats and rocky shore. (High tides during the fall and winter months are the best times to see grebes, ducks and other shorebirds near the shoreline.)

A paved path and a bike path parallel the beach (and Shoreline Drive).

DIRECTIONS: From I-980, exit on 11th/12th Streets, proceed through several traffic lights and make a left onto 5th Street, which leads to Broadway and the Oakland/Alameda Tube. Once through the Tube, you'll be traveling on Webster Street, which dead-ends at Central Avenue. Turn right on Central, then turn left on McKay Ave to reach the Crab Cove entrance.

THE HIKE: From the visitor center, join the paved walkway that leads along the edge of the mudflats of Crab Cove and past several large picnic areas. Check out a freshwater lagoon and a native plant garden and continue to board-sports rental concession.

The muddy shoreline gives way to sand strand and it's time to hit the beach. Pure beach-walking in the East Bay is at a premium, so enjoy! You'll find plenty of restrooms and drinking fountains en route.

The end of the hike is at the end of the beach, where it merges into the salt marsh located at the end of Park Street. Across the street from the shore is a McDonald's and a sushi restaurant.

Crown Beach: Saunter the sandy shore.

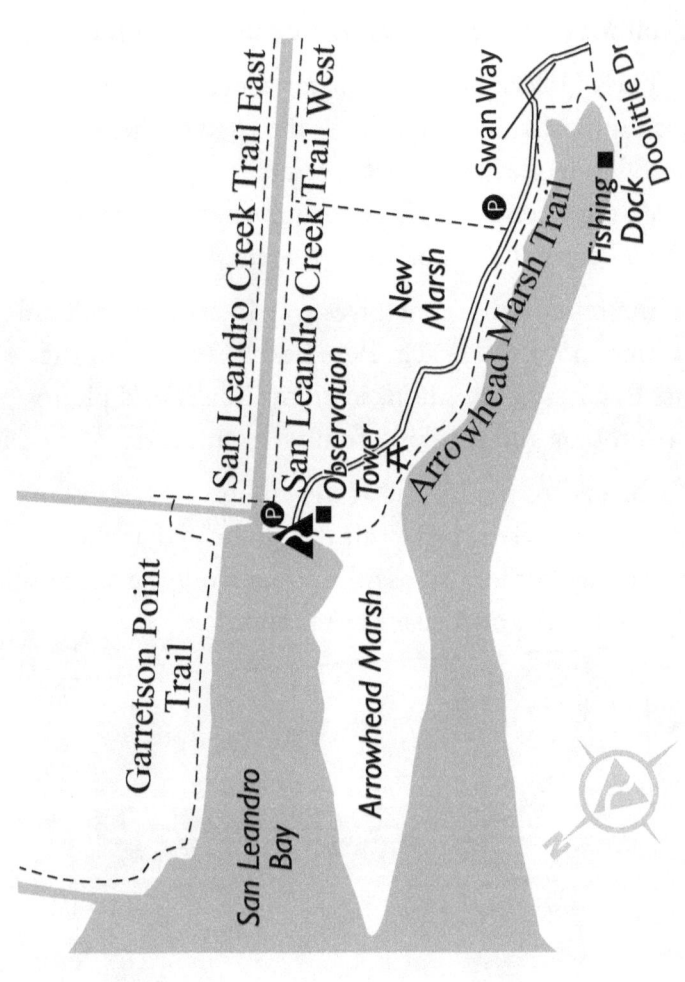

Martin Luther King Jr. Regional Shoreline

Arrowhead Marsh Trail

From Observation Tower to Fishing Dock is 2 miles round trip

Birds, lots of them, boardwalks, and bayside trails are the attractions of Martin Luther King Jr. Regional Shoreline that to the visitor can seem to be a curious combination of a municipal park and an island nature preserve. Surprisingly, this patch of protected marshland is located along the industrialized San Leandro Bay, and in close proximity to the Oakland Airport, Oakland Coliseum, and Interstate 880. (Construction of the airport, ballpark/football stadium, and freeway all but destroyed what was once prime wildlife habitat.)

The park originally opened as San Leandro Bay Regional Shoreline, and was renamed to honor the late civil rights leader. In 1998, the marshland restoration was completed. Shallow San Leandro

Bay is connected via narrow channels to San Francisco Bay. Crucial to the rehab effort was restoring tidal flow that was blocked because of the habitat-damaging filling-in activities that occurred during previous decades.

What a diversity of water birds and shorebirds! Shorebirds such as willets and stilts, diving ducks like scoters and buffleheads. Ruddy ducks, cinnamon teal, grebes, blue heron, widgeons, and the list goes on... The bird count (nearly 100 species) is especially high at the 741-acre park because of its location along the Pacific Flyway. Birdlife is most abundant from fall through spring.

Check out the birds from the paved flat trails, from a boardwalk that offers particularly good close-up views of the shorebirds, and from the observation tower overlooking Arrowhead Marsh.

Typical marshland flora includes lots of pickleweed and marsh grasses, plus fennel and sea fig. The gumplant, a tall thick-leaved plant that sports yellow, daisy-like flowers, splashes welcome color around the wetlands.

Among the easy-walking options is San Leandro Creek Trail (1.8 mile loop) which travels along the west bank and east bank of the creek, and Garreston Point Trail (1.4 mile round trip) honoring *Oakland Tribune* reporter Fred Garetson, whose stories spurred bay restoration efforts.

Arrowhead Marsh Trail explores the largest of the wetlands on San Leandro Bay. Along the trail look for the "Duplex Cone" sculpture by artist Roger Berry. The sun follows along the edge of the larger cone during summer solstice, and traces the edge of the smaller cone during winter solstice.

DIRECTIONS: From I-880 in Oakland, exit on Hegenberger Road. Head southwest 1 mile and turn right (north) on Doolittle Drive. In 0.25 mile, turn right on Swan Way then left into Martin Luther King Jr. Regional Shoreline. Follow the park road to the last lot at road's end.

THE HIKE: From the Observation Tower, join Arrowhead Marsh Trail and soon meet a boardwalk, which beckons you to walk across the marsh. Marsh and mudflats provide rich bird habitat.

Return to the trail and continue past a wide field, a favorite of Canada geese. Pass several picnic sites named for birds—egret, plover, kingfisher. The trail ends at a fishing dock.

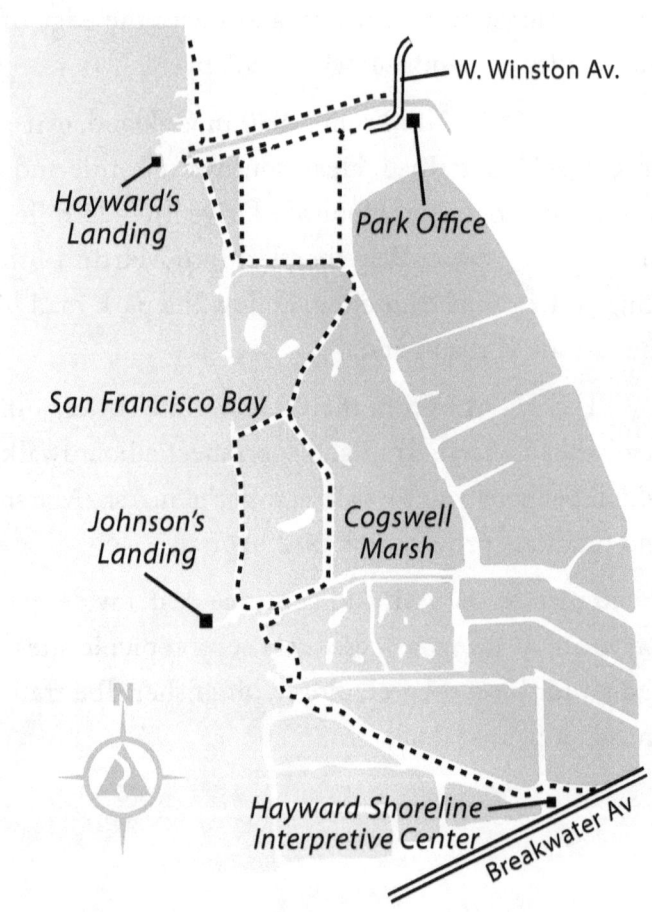

Hayward Regional Shoreline

Bay, Cogswell Marsh Trails

From Interpretive Center to Johnson's Landing with a loop around Cogswell Marsh is 3.5 miles round trip

Hike along narrow levees and across footbridges as you explore the shoreline, as well as freshwater and saltwater marshes in this 1,811-acre park, regarded as one of the best spots in the East Bay to view shorebirds. Clear-day vistas of human habitat are pretty good, too: Oakland Harbor, San Mateo Bridge, city of San Francisco.

Drop by the Hayward Shoreline Interpretive Center, then explore the shore from to Johnson's Landing (a onetime ferry stop). And don't miss the loop trail around Cogswell Marsh, a restored saltwater marsh that's habitat for nearly one hundred species of birds—great blue heron, western sandpiper, American avocet, marbled godwit, black-necked stilt, and so many more.

In the 19th century, levees were built in Hayward to create land for salt production. During the 1980s, major ecological rehab efforts transformed the former commercial salt flats and its evaporation ponds back into viable marshes and wildlife habitat.

Cogswell Marsh, once salt works barriers were removed, dikes breached, and tidal action restored, rebounded rapidly to become a functioning salt marsh. The restoration project is a fine example of what can transpire when, with help from humans, nature is given the chance to heal itself. The marsh is named for Dr. Howard Cogswell, a retired professor of environmental biology at Cal State University Hayward, who led the way to create the park and restore the wetlands.

Hayward Marsh was also quite a restoration effort: five ponds and 15 islands were created as habitat for nesting birds. Treated wastewater is released into the marsh; water flows and levels are controlled by a series of valves and channels.

This 3.5 mile partial loop through marshes and shoreline is an easy hike on perfectly flat trail along the bay and across a series of levies. For a longer hike, continue north on Bay Trail to San Leandro Marina.

Hiking the marsh trails here is a quieter, more contemplative experience than walking the busier and more urban pathways found in other East Bay regional shorelines. Narrow levees and bridges just seem to take you away from it all. For a wet and wild experience, come when it's windy and the waves are high!

Hayward Regional Shoreline

DIRECTIONS: From eastbound Highway 92 in Hayward, at the east end of the San Mateo Bridge, exit on Clawiter Road and cross over the highway. Make a left onto Breakwater Avenue and follow it for about a mile as it bends left and right then parallels the highway. Find roadside parking near the Hayward Shoreline Interpretive Center.

THE HIKE: From behind the visitor center, join the wide dirt path and walk west. You're sure to see many species of shorebirds as you hike past HARD Marsh and Hayward Marsh. In about 0.9 mile, reach the bayshore, where the trail turns north. Enjoy clear-day views across the water to San Francisco and Oakland. The trail crosses a slough, meanders the western shore of Hayward Marsh and arrives at a junction at about the 1.1-mile mark.

Go left to begin the loop around Cogswell Marsh, and soon reach Johnson's Landing, a small cove with a beach and breakwater. Behold the sweep of the Alameda Country shoreline as well as Cogswell Marsh and its busy birds.

Cross a bridge over a gap in the levee as the trail bends east. At a second bridge, the trail splits again. (For a longer hike, cross the bridge and hike northeast to Triangle Marsh and Hayward's Landing.) Begin the return trip by walking a dike across Cogswell Marsh. After 0.5 mile, bend right with the trail onto another dike that leads back to the bayshore near Johnson's Landing. Retrace your steps back to the visitor center.

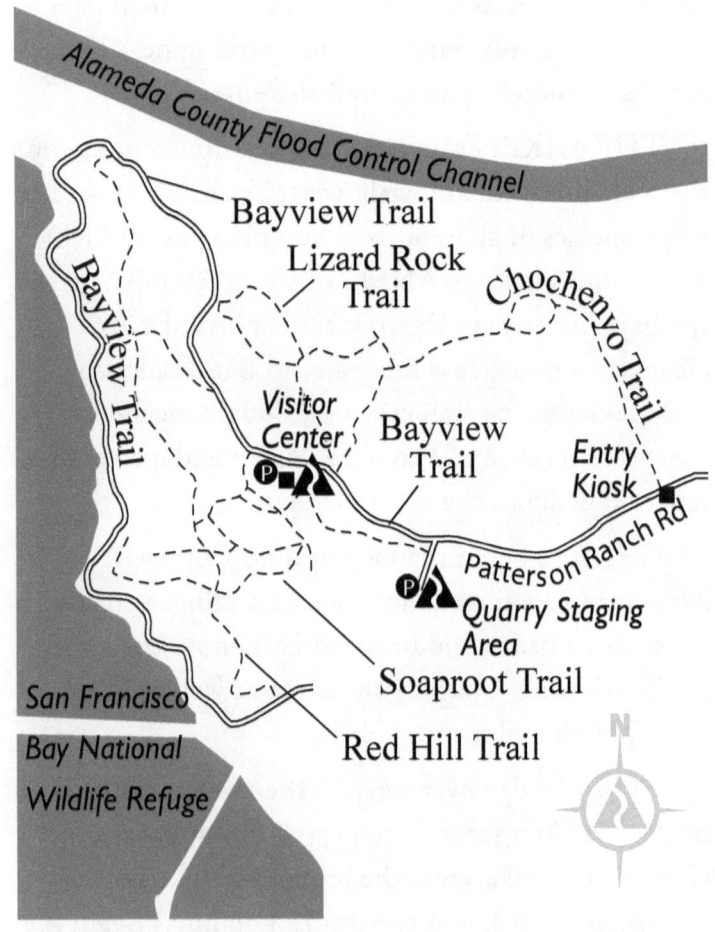

Coyote Hills Regional Park

Bayview and 6 more trails

4.75-mile loop with 250-foot elevation gain

Roam the hills and marshlands of a sprawling wetland, located where Alameda Creek flows into San Francisco Bay. Coyote Hills Regional Park is a great place to observe shorebirds galore and many a rabbit and squirrel in the grassy hills.

Waters south and west of the park are part of the San Francisco Bay National Wildlife Refuge.(See hike description in this guide.)

The trail network includes the 3.5-mile, multiuse, Bayview Trail, a paved loop that leads by salt ponds and along the bay. Highlights are views of the bay, the hills and marshlands. Red Hill Trail is a must; it leads to park high point, 292-foot Red Hill.

The park has a dozen named trails from Muskrat to Lizard Rock to Glider Hill, which sounds complicated, but these trails are well signed; fear not, you won't get lost. You will stay interested, though, because the park is large and varied enough to offer a good hike. A loop hike from Quarry Staging Area is one way to go; you can also begin your exploration at the visitor center and fashion shorter or longer loops.

Check out the nature and wildlife exhibits at Coyote Hills Visitor Center, and the Possum's Pocket Nature Store. Park interpretive efforts focus on the East Bay's original inhabitants, the native Ohlone. Shell mound sites (2,000 years old), along with re-creations of a tule reed boat and a family house, tell the story of the Ohlone, who lived well off the bounty of the bay and nearby hills. Nineteenth- and twentieth-century enterprises along the shore were many and varied: a farm, a ranch, a dairy, rock quarry, duck hunting club, and Nike missile site.

DIRECTIONS: From I-880 in Fremont, take Highway 84 west and exit on Paseo Padre Parkway. (Heading eastbound on Highway 84, Paseo Padre is the first exit after the toll plaza.) Drive north 1 mile, turn left on Patterson Ranch Road and drive another mile to Coyote Hills Regional Park. Continue past the entry kiosk to parking at Quarry Staging Area or a bit farther to road's end and parking by the visitor center.

THE HIKE: From Quarry Staging Area, cross the entry road and go right on paved Tuibun Trail.

After 0.5 mile, reach the entry kiosk and go left on Chochenyo Trail meandering north then west alongside D.U.S.T. Marsh, and past Tuibun Village Site.

Join Lizard Rock Trail and follow it 0.25 mile to Bayview Trail. Pass by Red Hill Trail (for now) and travel northwest then bend south on Bayview Trail for a pleasant mile along the bay shore to Soap Plant Trail, a 0.3-mile long connector to Red Hill Trail. Now comes a bit of climbing, first to a breezy peak known for obvious reasons as Glider Hill, then to the top of Red Hill.

Enjoy the great views from this promontory and descend Red Hill Trail to Nike Trail, following this path 0.25 mile back to Bayview Trail, which leads alongside Main Marsh to the visitor center, and returns you to the trailhead.

Roam the Coyote Hills and get great Bay views.

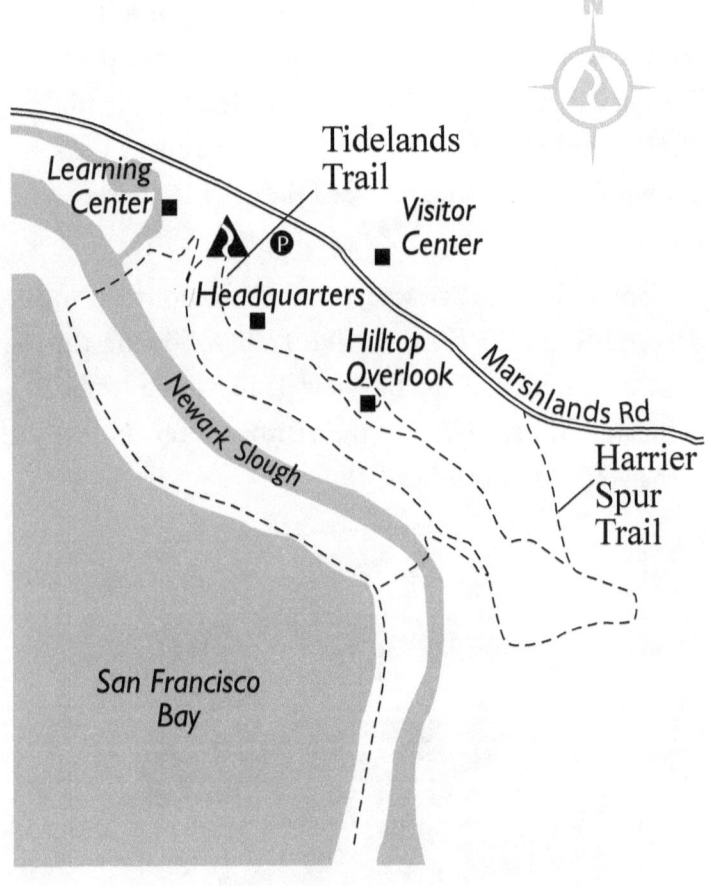

San Francisco Bay National Wildlife Refuge

Tidelands Trail

1.6 miles round trip.

San Francisco Bay National Wildlife Refuge is a big one, befitting the West Coast's most crucial bay and marsh tidewaters, salt ponds and mudflats. At more than 23,000 acres, it's the nation's largest urban wildlife refuge, critical habitat for the more than 280 species of birds counted here.

Thirty miles of trail trace the bay shore. Some of these pathways use the tops of levees to cross mud flats and salt ponds. (Note that the levees are created of mud dredged from the bay and are sometimes closed for repairs, or for the seasonal use of nesting waterfowl.)

Interpretive paths, complete with trailside panels, offer easy-to-follow lessons about the bay's fish, fowl and coastal ecology. One refuge trail even travels to Coyote Hills Regional Park by way of a foot and bicycle bridge over the Dumbarton Bridge toll plaza.

Tidelands Trail is a wide, levee-top interpretive path that visits marsh and bay wetlands. Bay views are grand from a hilltop overlook. Tidelands Trail, honored with National Recreation Trail status, loops around Newark Slough, visits a salt company pumphouse-turned-picnic site, and offers a duck blind from which to shoot birds (with a camera of course!).

Drop by the attractive visitor center perched on a rise overlooking the restored La Riviere Marsh. Pick up a trail map, check out the exhibits and inquire about the refuge's schedule of guided walks and interpretive programs.

Choose a loop on Tidelands Trail and add the short climb to Hilltop Overlook or hike the 5-mile loop on Newark Slough Trail, which circles a series of salt ponds. The path definitely has its moments, and offers views that open up west to the Santa Cruz Mountains, and when you head east, Mission Peak pops into view.

I'd rate Newark Slough Trail higher, but must report that traffic noise from Highway 84 is both constant and jarring.

DIRECTIONS: From Highway 84 at the east end of Dumbarton Bridge, exit on Thornton Avenue (first exit after toll plaza) and drive southwest 0.75 mile to the Refuge entrance on the right and follow signs to parking. The visitor center is located near the first parking to your right. Join Tidelands Trail from the second parking lot on the left.

Tidelands Trail descends to the edge of the marsh then crosses a bridge over Newark Slough, intersects Newark Slough Trail and joins a levee.

Stroll past salt company salt evaporator ponds, home to brine shrimp and the birds that eat them. A duck hunter's cabin and a duck blind gives you a chance to learn how ducks were sighted in the pre-refuge past and how they're sighted in the refuge today.

Nearby is a salt industry pumphouse, built on piles over the water; it's now a truly unique picnic shelter. After re-crossing Newark Slough on another bridge, the trail returns to the parking area.

Tidelands Trail leads past a duck hunters' cabin—holdover from another era when ducks were shot with guns, not cameras.

Discover More Day Hikes and Bay Hikes!

HIKE THE SOUTH BAY
Best Day Hikes in the South Bay
and Along the Peninsula

HIKE SAN FRANCISCO
Best Day Hikes in the Golden Gate
National Parklands and Around the City

HIKE POINT REYES
Best Day Hikes in
Point Reyes National Seashore

"John McKinney tells the grand tale of the California coast like no one before him has done."

—Thomas Rigler, Executive Producer, *City Walk* and *California Coastal Trail* (PBS)

Hiking on the Edge: Dreams, Schemes, and 1600 Miles on the California Coastal Trail

A saga, a celebration, a comedy, a lament, this narrative ranks with the classics of California travel literature.

All of John McKinney's books, including HIKE Point Reyes, are available from TheTrailmaster.com

THETRAILMASTER.COM

- Tips
- Tours
- Trails
- Tales

JOHN MCKINNEY

John McKinney is an award-winning writer, public speaker, and author of 30 hiking-themed books: inspiring narratives, top-selling guides, books for children.

John is particularly passionate about sharing the stories of California trails. He is the only one to have visited—and written about—all 280 California State Parks. John tells the story of his epic hike along the entire California coast in the critically acclaimed *Hiking on the Edge: Dreams, Schemes, and 1600 Miles on the California Coastal Trail*.

For 18 years John, aka The Trailmaster, wrote a weekly hiking column for the Los Angeles Times, and has hiked and enthusiastically told the story of more than 10 thousand miles of trail across California and around the world. His "Every Trail Tells a Story" series of guides highlight the very best hikes in California.

The intrepid Eagle Scout has written more than a thousand stories and opinion pieces about hiking, parklands, and our relationship with nature.

A passionate advocate for hiking and our need to reconnect with nature, John is a frequent public speaker, and shares his tales on radio, on video, and online.

JOHN MCKINNEY:
"EVERY TRAIL TELLS A STORY."

HIKE ON.

TheTrailmaster.com

www.ingramcontent.com/pod-product-compliance
Lightning Source LLC
Chambersburg PA
CBHW030445300426
44112CB00009B/1164